MW01206532

Love and ~~Dating for Shy~~

People

Hard Hitting Advice for Naturally Introverted Men and Women

www.developedlife.com (Master Yourself, Master Life)

The Developed Life Love and Dating Series

The "Fire Lotus" Seal of Quality

Special Message: Thank you for your purchase of "Love and Dating for Shy People". I try to maintain quality in the production of my books. This is because of a disappointing trend in the self-publishing world where cheap, outsourced books are mass-produced by marketing firms. They are often unedited or with poor grammar, yet are passed off as real products. It's up to both readers and writers to keep the market quality and spam-free.

Free Supplemental Booklet: Right now you can check out www.developedlife.com/subscribe and receive a free copy of the booklet **"10 Success Techniques to Master Your Life"** for those who desire to create optimal life philosophies. This is an important resource to have alongside this book.

Table of Contents

Disclaimer: 1

Introduction 6

Before We Get Started 7

Chapter One – "Introvert" Tendencies 8

So What is an Introvert? 11

Adding Extroverted Tendencies When Necessary...... 13

The Common Sticking Points 14

Curing These Awkward Social Traits.................... 17

Exercise: Take Them Off a Pedestal! 22

Chapter Two – Breaking the Ice 25

Where and How to Meet People......................... 26

Making a Presentation.. 29

What to Do Next 31

I Don't Know What to Talk About........................ 34

Help, I've Been Rejected!.................................... 36

Chapter Summary 39

HEY! Are you skimming these pages? Slow down a sec, hot-rod. . 40

Chapter Three – Flirting and Body Language........ 42

Are You Flirting Enough? 43

Should I Be a Flirt? Body Language Attraction Cues.......... 44

Women Showing Interest to Men 46

Men Showing Interest to Women 47

The Relationship Between Humor and Flirting........ 49

Humor on Dates.. 49

What Humor Style is Right for the Two of You?...... 53

Negative Relationship Patterning........................ 54

Chapter Summary and the Big Point 57

Chapter Four – On Dating Logistics 58

Ignore Most Conventional Ideas 58

What Does This Mean For You? 60

So, How Do I Ask That Cutie Out? 62

Making the Date Work, and Making a Move 65

About Making the First Move 67

"Let's Just Be Friends" 71

Moving to the Next Level 74

Chapter Summary 75

Chapter Five – Limiting Beliefs and Dating Falsehoods 77

When Sex and Dating is About Power Versus Love 77

Some Proposed Solutions 81

The Dangers of Needing Validation and Approval 85

The Ten Percent Disease 87

Misc. Negative Opinions About Sex and Dating 89

Chapter Summary 93

Chapter Six – Online Dating Ins and Outs 94

The Immediate Problem With Online Dating 94

The Online Dating Landscape 95

And Herein Lies the Problem With Online Dating 99

A System of Appearances: Is It Worth It? 100

Why Meeting in Person is Superior 101

How Online Dating Can Actually Work 102

Chapter Seven – Help, I Still Can't Find a Date! 104

Chapter Eight – Dating Worst Case Scenario Checklist 109

Final Thoughts 114

Related Books by Cyrus Thomson.. 116

Free E-Book and Newsletter 117

About the Author.. 117

Introduction

Welcome to *Love and Dating for Shy People*. My name is Cyrus, and as a part-time dating and relationship coach for a number of years, I've been desiring for some time to create a product that helps out we introverts who are trying to navigate what can be an intimidating world for so many.

My paradigm writing this is the big city; and in a metropolis, many of the problems people face in love and romance are extrapolated. There's more people, it's more hectic, more expensive, and there can be a sense of judgment that can intimidate us as we search for partners and lovers.

And to make an already difficult situation worse; in the 21st century people are now collectively distracted. Meeting people is far too often supplanted for staying at home on a Friday night on Facebook. If one has a tendency toward shyness, the distractions and excuses not to leave the apartment are innumerable.

And then, we also have the common issue of our schedules. "I don't have the time to *date* anyone," people commonly complain. And, it's true. Career minded people may work very long hours—and if you're planted somewhere like the healthcare field where 80 hour work weeks are standard—just forget it!

However, I believe that "shyness" is not some type of mental condition where it's impossible to change habits or begin mingling. As we'll explore in this book, there are methods to curb dating fears, while at the same time ensuring that your tendency toward cerebral activities does not get in your way. This way, you can be both introverted AND social, with an active love life.

Before We Get Started

First of all, thank you for your purchase. Let's go over a couple of things before we delve in.

If you're like me, you like to skim. Although this type of book can be picked up at any point, you won't experience many results if you gloss over large parts. Some topics need to be absorbed and even put into physical practice before they are worth anything to you. So, don't be lazy about this.

Additionally, if you want to reach out to me, just send me a note at cyrus@developedlife.com. I can answer questions or help with any of the areas of this book. I pretty much always reply to people's inquiries.

With all of that out of the way let's get started.

Chapter One – "Introvert" Tendencies

At the very beginning of this book, I'd like to point out the reason why I prefer the term "shy people" and not "introvert", and why I may write "introvert" with quotation marks around it. The reason is because I've grown skeptical that these terms are even accurate; as have others in the psychology community[1] who argue that Jung's original terms are way too black and white to be applied as actual social models.

The problem with the term introvert, or when comparing it to the extrovert, is that it immediately creates a form of limited thinking. Examples may include, "I'm an introvert, that's why I'm home tonight." Or, "I'm introverted, so I'd best not go talk to that guy / girl across the room."

---

[1] http://www.psychologytoday.com/blog/the-buddha-was-introvert/201404/there-is-no-such-thing-introvert-or-extrovert

Traditionally and according to Jung, an introvert is known as somebody whose locus of consciousness is their own mind and emotions. By contrast, an extrovert is connected to the emotions, feelings and thoughts of others. What this means is that an extrovert enters a social situation disconnected from excessive personal thought, and is immediately engaged to people around him or her. However, an introvert could also be the "wallflower" of the room, thinking about him or herself to a point that's a bit excessive.

An introvert may find him or herself more satisfied with mental, cerebral pursuits. While an extrovert may require constant social stimulation, an introvert can achieve the same type of stimulation from reading a book, writing in a journal, playing a game, or any number of activities that may or may not involve other people.

Nobody really claims one personality is better than the other, but there's a type of consensus that introverts struggle more in social areas, and in the worst examples personify the "40 year old virgin" as made famous by Hollywood.

Fortunately, there are some reasons to be skeptical of these terms.

- An extrovert may possess introvert qualities.

- In fact, it's absolutely verified a person can be both an extrovert AND an introvert.

- An introverted mood may change to an extroverted mood with some training and practice.

- A very extroverted person may successfully adapt to a job or school curriculum that requires introverted habits, such as quiet study-time and other mental pursuits.

- Likewise, many so-called introverts hold public positions and require being in the social spotlight to an even greater degree than what a party-going extrovert may be used to—and they may succeed even more.

So What <u>is</u> an Introvert?

If this model is outdated, how can we instead classify an introvert?

A good definition could be as follows: **an introvert gains as much, or more, pleasure from "cerebral" activities than his or her peers, and sees no trouble swapping social activities for mental ones.**

That means anyone who is a writer or creative type could very likely be introverted in this sense.

It does not, however, mean that an introvert is naturally inhibited socially. **Instead, an introvert simply has different priorities, but is more than adaptable to becoming social when necessary.**

It's clear that both of these terms, as they're commonly imagined in the black and white sense, are useless—as the human personality is too flexible and ever-evolving for anybody to be classified in these very limiting ways.

Perhaps the main issue is that introverts are often confused as having a very separate and unrelated issue; the problem of a **social anxiety disorder**, also known as being agoraphobic.

Social phobias could be the result of a number of factors, such as:

-      Chronic self-consciousness or self-esteem issues.

-      A byproduct of a body dysmorphic disorder (obsession with physical appearance).

-     Uncontrolled anxiety in crowds, triggered by a complex post-traumatic stress disorder.

Deeply rooted social phobias are another topic entirely. The more complex ones require a lot of effort to cure. It's not the intention of this book to solve such a serious problem.

The issue at hand—as it relates to your romantic life—is that of being *shy*. It is a natural tendency for people to have *mild* levels of social anxiety and difficulties interacting. These are the types of issues that we can try to solve in this program.

So, before you check yourself in to the state mental hospital and classify yourself as unfit for normal human interaction, consider that your problems may be very mild.

In fact, many of the conditions that are formally classified in the Diagnostic and Statistical Manual of Mental Disorders (DSM) can appear in any of us to a mild degree. For instance, with body dysmorphic disorder, this may manifest mildly in an otherwise mentally healthy woman who changes her dress three times before she goes out.

(The more severe examples of such a situation are those who undergo chronic, unhealthy amounts of plastic surgery, or are completely afraid to leave their houses because of fear of being judged for a perceived physical flaw.)

Shyness is most likely the result of mild social phobias and things that can be tackled if such traits are interfering with your romantic prospects. Otherwise, an introverted nature is not something set in stone, and those tendencies to seek inward satisfaction can, by all means, become a strength of yours—and never a weakness.

If, on the other hand, your feelings are more severe—and the prospect of even going outside of the house creates intense anxiety, then consider some type of serious professional help, along with a more advanced program to help you (you can try the _30 Day Social Anxiety Bootcamp_).

Adding Extroverted Tendencies When Necessary

As it appears that nobody is forced to assume the role of an introvert—or an extrovert—certain tendencies can be added as social habits to help counter-balance excessively mental priorities. Here are some examples:

- **Eating Alone Versus With a Group:** If you are somebody whom chooses to dine by him or herself, this means you are missing out on what could be important social interaction. If you take lunch breaks at work, and you tend to disappear— then instead find colleagues, or preferably people you haven't met before.

- **Introducing Formally:** Another trait of "introverts" (shy people) is to withhold introductions, or to feel self-conscious before formally representing oneself. Instead, resist this urge and get into the habit of being the first to extend a hand and say your name. The introduction process, integral to any culture, exists because it immediately puts people at ease, and is considered the first step to getting to know someone better.

• **Introducing Others:** An extrovert gains satisfaction from social feedback, and so it's common for extroverts to seek to be inclusive, as this generates positive social feedback among everybody. Making it a point to introduce new people to one another also helps everyone feel more comfortable around the introducer.

• **Choosing to Go Out:** Finally, one of the biggest differences is that, as an introvert, you may be inclined to stay home most nights, and the reason is because naturally you gain the same satisfaction and pleasure from solo activities, whether it's reading, writing, watching movies, or anything that plays with your imagination. However, as nothing is stopping you from embracing extroverted qualities, it's possible to channel some of your enthusiasm for free time into the pleasures that can be obtained from meeting and interacting with people. With some discipline, you can begin a regiment of leaving the house and spending that free time among fellow humans.

The Common Sticking Points

It would be a nice if it were so simple for a wallflower to immediately start mingling and having fun, but there are some very common negative thought patterns that often get in the way. Here's a brief list—consider which ones apply the most to you.

Disconnection: This is the phenomenon when a person feels that they cannot associate with a social group. It's the common feeling of "not fitting in" that may be exacerbated during high school, but persists into adulthood.

Social disconnection is a symptom of a self-esteem problem, and possibly even a major inferiority complex. It means a person assumes they are unworthy of a group's attention. Feelings of being "left out" are common. The situation gets worse when a group of people—let's say a group of co-workers or classmates—feel uncomfortable by that person's insecurity, and they begin isolating him or her from activities or regular discussion. This may perpetuate a feeling of social exclusion, confirming his or her original paranoia.

Physical Flaw Insecurities: Earlier we mentioned body dysmorphic disorders and how this may manifest in a mild way when someone changes their dress multiple times before feeling comfortable to leave the door. Another mild manifestation of this syndrome is if you are overly concerned about a physical flaw or perceived imperfection, and it creates a sudden sense of shyness before socializing.

This can be especially destabilizing to a person's love life, as it could also go hand-in-hand with a fear that a potential love interest will be disinterested. Some common factors include weight, age and symmetry.

Lack of Social Skills: Although rarely is this a problem in itself (as it usually is the result of one of the above related issues), some people have simple difficulty forming conversations. They find themselves assailed by "awkward silences", pauses, and an uncertainty about how to carry on a conversation. This may develop into a general fear of

15

approaching new people, as they are worried about dealing with these same negative feelings.

Too High Expectations: Especially in the context of dating, this is a very big issue. A common problem I see is that people enter a social context desperately *wanting* to walk away with a date or some type of romantic success. This behavior is very detrimental because the other parties can sense an agenda is present. This may turn an interaction very awkward, especially if a person senses a strong, premature interest toward him or her. Repeated rejections could then lead to a persistent social phobia.

Too Low Expectations: Conversely, it's possible to have very low expectations of people that you meet. It's hard to make new friends, let alone new lovers, if a person believes that there is no evolution of acquaintance, to friend, to something more. This lack of interest in people can persist as a type of shyness in its own right.

Intimidation: Logically, there is very little reason to be intimidated by any other person unless that person outranks you in some type of military hierarchy. However, being intimidated is very common—especially when one person puts another on an undeserving pedestal. All too often, I see this occur among men who feel a woman, because of her physically attractive features, is out of his so-called "league".

Curing These Awkward Social Traits

In the common vernacular, all of these traits can be interpreted as being "socially awkward", which is a catch-all term for any socially uncertain behavior (most of which have roots in the sticking points mentioned before).

So, are there any true methods to start eliminating these behaviors and increase one's social confidence? While there are many different causative factors for the sticking points, there are just a few strategies that might create some immediate positive results. These work best if you're willing to be open-minded and change your way of thinking about some fundamental topics:

Relax About the Outcome: Usually the reason someone feels awkward or persistently shy is because they're placing too much emphasis on a social interaction. In other words, they feel it's so important that they overthink every nuance. They worry if their conversational partner is losing interest, they worry about what they're thinking of them, and they worry about the end results. Will they get a phone number? A friend? A date? Something more?

This is what happens when an introverted or mentally centered personality enters a social situation. One of the core skills that determines strong social skills is the ability to relax and simply forget many of these tendencies to over-think the situation.

The reason is because conversation or any type of interaction depends on a mutual exchange of *energy and information*. Despite what we may believe, our thoughts are far less "silent" than we imagine. Whatever we're thinking is going to be revealed in our body language, subtle cues and through our partner's intuitive sense. All of these factors give away what's going on in our minds.

This is why "creepy" people stay "creepy" no-matter what they say. It's why it's hard to hide excitement, and why people automatically can tell when you're sad or upset, even if you think you're hiding it so cleverly.

As a result of this, **it's a lot easier to just "let go" and reveal your thoughts and actions without pausing constantly to over-analyze and censor yourself.** The very act of "over thinking" a social situation means that you're in your head, believing foolishly that your thoughts are safe from the world. They're not.

So, practice "not thinking" the next time you socialize. If something's on your mind, just say it. The thinking happens as you're talking—those *are* your thoughts. If you attempt to make this basic process any more complex, then you can expect a lot of that "social awkwardness" to rear its ugly head.

And, this is a skill. Remember, an introvert must learn the *skill set* of an extrovert, so relax if you don't get it right the first time—it's the type of thing that take practice.

Are You Judging People? Another thing that may make a person feel hesitant to engage in a social situation is the habit (and yes, it's a habit, just like smoking), of judging people. Usually, the more concerned a person is that they're being judged—the more they are, in fact, the ones who are actually judging.

The truth is that people are surprisingly cognizant of "judgers" and generally respond by reciprocating judgmental behavior (creating the ever common vicious circle).

So, if you have some idea in your mind that certain classes of people, based on any factor, deserve to be second-guessed before you speak to them, you're setting yourself up for a lot of uncomfortable moments. Again, just because you think those thoughts are private, does NOT mean they really are. This is why bigots, classists, racists and sexists find their social lives are so mysteriously barren.

Pivot: If a conversation isn't going anywhere, like the two of you are droning on about the weather and you begin to feel uncomfortable—the odds are your conversational partner feels awkward, as well. This is where the art of "pivoting" comes into play, which is the power to switch a conversation seamlessly to another topic.

This is surprisingly easy to do IF you practice. If you're talking about the weather, try pivoting to something in the environment, like an observation about the place you're in, or a story from earlier in the day. Whatever it is, the idea is just to keep sharing information and try something that is more enjoyable anytime the current thread is going dull.

It's a tic-for-tac process, and in addition there's no pressure to keep any conversation going indefinitely. It's very important to take such pressure and expectations off the table. If the conversation feels like it needs to finish— then let it come to a halt naturally. Go somewhere else or talk to somebody different, and catch up with that person later.

This is another reason why it's good to avoid dates where you are forced to just keep talking to each other (like dinner at a restaurant)—but we'll get to that later in this book.

Energy Levels: Sometimes the main thing that can switch you from a state of shyness or social anxiety, to general competence and relaxation is your energy level. Although a separate book could be written about this topic, some important things to consider are:

Your diet: If you are eating a lot of simple carbs throughout the day, it becomes VERY hard to socialize because your body is trying to process all that nasty refined sugar. You will lose energy levels at random points and it will affect your mood. This may hinder your abilities at even basic socializing.

Sleep: It's also very hard to even feel motivated to talk to people if you are perpetually exhausted. Not sleeping has a large part to do with bad scheduling. If after work, you are up late dealing with other responsibilities, it means you need to find a way to get more done in less time—and give yourself an hour before bed to unwind and get a full night's rest.

Exercise: If you don't jog, use machines, or perform pushups / sit-ups—you're missing out on more than just calorie shedding. Exercise keeps energy levels high and affects your mood throughout the day.

Make a Singular Goal of Providing Happiness

This sounds a bit hippy-ish, doesn't it? Well, read on because it's the most important advice I was ever taught about socializing.

A lot of people enter social situations with conscious—or subconscious—motivations to "get" things like value, affection, or acceptance. However, the more you desire from people in a social context, the more that you project a feeling of discomfort.

If your only motivation is to brighten people up a little bit, maybe you tell a joke or you are just a pleasant listener, then you project a feeling of relaxation. That is, you are giving people the feelings of acceptance that *they* desire, and lessening any type of tension caused by the burden of wanting things out of them.

You may want to ask yourself if, on a subconscious level, you seek to extract value from people you meet. This could range from fishing for compliments, to subtly boasting about your accomplishments from a position of desiring respect.

A simple shift in attitude can correct this. Instead of seeking compliments, try providing them. Instead of boasting about your accomplishments, show interest in other people's works. This one behavioral shift can open up a lot of doors you never imagined.

Exercise: Take Them Off a Pedestal!

Because we assign undo value to people based on things like appearance, sex appeal and status, it's a good idea to start deprogramming yourself from this type of thinking. This is especially important for your dating life; I want you to imagine the most attractive, highest-status representative of somebody you'd find as a romantic prospect. Maybe it's someone like actress Yvonne Strahovski:

... Or Tom Brady.

You might be placing a lot of value on these people because they look sexy, are undoubtedly wealthy, and overall more important than you think you are.

How would you feel if you encountered one of them at a cocktail party? Would your legs turn to mush? Would you be paralyzed with fear? Would you turn into an amoeba and slither back to the ocean from whence you came?

Now, do you ever act like this among people who are not Yvonne or Tom? But just strangers whom you randomly encounter, and yet feel very nervous to talk to?

It's (once again) the problem of putting people on pedestals who don't deserve to be there. As you explore human psychology, some fundamental truths become apparent, namely that any decent person, regardless of background, will appreciate the company of somebody who makes them feel good.

So whether it's Strahovski, Brady, Clooney, Johansson, or a regular non-celebrity who just happens to be attractive and "intimidating" to you, I want you to visualize approaching them. Imagine talking to them and feeling no sense of intimidation. You must believe that you're an equal.

Imagine talking for a good amount of time, with no sudden rejection or them excusing themselves. Imagine what it feels like being in rapport with a good friend. Now, imagine that friend is an attractive stranger who you've just met.

It's important to begin training and re-conditioning your mind to see people as equals, and forget about social conditions and rules that some people are more important than you are. In reality, most of these conventions are myths, and they only become real if somebody believes they're real.

Show me a beautiful famous person, and I'll show you someone who has the same insecurities and loneliness that can affect any human.

Chapter Two – Breaking the Ice

The last chapter was effectively a primer for getting out of your shell and changing some of your beliefs about meeting people. Meeting others is the core of dating, and it's something shy people may have difficulties with. In this chapter, I hope to make the process easier for you.

The reason is that the first step in dating is meeting people. Typically the process goes: encountering a stranger, talking, feeling a personal connection, a friendship, and then some type of physically romantic trigger (such as kissing, petting, or a sexual activity) that establishes a dating or relationship dynamic.

This chain of events can be thought of as a linear process. You can't meet people if you don't leave the house. You can't make a friend if you don't talk to that person and make a connection. And, you can't establish a romantic dynamic if the two of you avoid kissing or other intimate behaviors.

Where and How to Meet People

The first thing to do is throw out ideas made popular in Hollywood movies. And if you're a guy, I'd forget most men's dating advice that suggests going to bars and nightclubs; including the various tactics recommended to get attention in those places.

You actually want to avoid any location where the dynamic is dating, singles, or being "on the hunt". This sounds counter-intuitive, but there are many reasons why it's a bad idea to go to nightclubs or even singles mixers.

-       In clubs and bars, it's expected for men to approach women. As a result, women are on edge and more defensive.

-       If you're a guy in such an environment, the high pressure will make basic conversation much more intimidating. In addition, due to the large amount of competition, most women are forced to size up guys based on split-second factors or superficial qualities.

-       If you're a woman in such a place, you won't be meeting men who are behaving as their true selves, rather you'll only see their "club personas". This is when a guy is trying to be impressive and comes across as awkward, insecure, and trying too hard.

-       The loud music literally blocks meaningful conversation. So along with all of the other challenges—you have to make a connection while fighting past deafness.

-        Finally, if you're a "shy person", while it's good to go outside of your comfort zone, don't make life harder than it should be by forcing yourself to try and meet people in an environment that you can't relax in. Most shy, "introverted" people desire mental stimuli, and they simply don't find that in nightclubs or busy party atmospheres. It is, however, easier to experience this through stimulating conversation and a pleasant atmosphere in a daytime setting, or anywhere that's a bit more quiet.

So, I've compiled a list of some places that I think would be very adequate for meeting people and potentially finding a romantic partner (or two).

•   **Non-Dating Related Meetups:** Take the pressure off by going to Meetup.com or Craigslist community events unrelated to dating. For instance, book clubs, hiking clubs, etc. These are geared for people who just moved to your city, and want to expand their social circles. Naturally, single people do show up to these events.

•   **Group Related Social Mixers:** One of the best place to meet people are parties and events where there's a common denominator. For instance, if you belong to an art group, and it's the opening of a new gallery. This provides immediate ways to "break the ice". In addition, there's a lot less pressure as you meet people in this type of non-dating related dynamic.

•   **Social Circle Events:** A house party among friends or within a close community is a perfect example of a social circle event. There are fewer barriers between people, because most people are friends of one another. This is an excellent way to make connections without any of the usual social pressure one may feel among total strangers.

•   **Industry Events:** I don't suggest dating co-workers. However, whatever your profession might be, it doubtlessly has other people passionate about similar things, which means very little effort spent on finding commonalities and performing introductory small talk.

As you can see, the idea is to take the pressure off of approaching a stranger. Many people suffer hard in this area. And it's understandable, even people without chronic shyness (or full-fledged social phobia) find approaching strangers difficult.

The best strategy to deal with this always involves taking the coldness of the first encounter out of the equation. While it's not impossible to meet somebody that you really connect with while you're in line at a coffee shop; inherent obstructions exist, like the fact the two of you might be rushing to go to separate workplaces and altogether not feeling very social.

These types of "cold" meetings can feel high-pressure for virtually anybody. In my experience as a dating coach in Los Angeles, I've seen a lot of advice from coaches on both sides of the gender aisle (but primarily among men) that encourages people to approach strangers in public settings.

Sometimes this works out, obviously. My parents met this way, as have many other couples I know. However, it can also be very grueling. Outside of those perfect moment opportunities, trying to break through someone's shell and make a real connection without catching them off guard or appearing "try hard" can be a real challenge.

So, make the process easier on yourself by allowing the environment to naturally break the ice. Always the easiest ice breaker is the context of a situation. If for instance an opera just finished, the context would be "What did you think of that opera?". In other settings the context could range from mutual enjoyment of a sport or activity, or the fact that the two of you are connected by a mutual friend (e.g.: "Oh, you're Bill's friend. Hi, I'm…").

By seeking out these "warm" approach opportunities, it's just a lot easier for everybody.

Making a Presentation

Although personality goes most of the way; we have to be realistic about the nature of meeting potential dates; looks and presentation matter.

First of all, you shouldn't freak out about things you cannot control. Probably since you were young and in school, you've felt the pressure about factors like facial symmetry and weight (girls) and muscles, height and, er, appendage size (boys).

As we leave the schoolyard and become adults, these factors become less critically important; except among very looks-centric clubbing and party scenes (that I'm guessing you want to avoid, anyway).

However, if you make no effort at all to at least look your best according to *you*, then you will lose any sense of allure or sex appeal, which will work against you.

I do think it's important to at least handle the critical factors: diet, exercise, skin care. If you're like me—a genetically skinny guy—you're probably not going to become Mr. Universe no matter how hard you try, so don't stress about going to the gym 8 hours a day to impress some non-existent girl.

However, some weight training won't hurt, combined with balancing out your diet—avoiding greasy, fatty foods that also affect your skin. Increase your amount of protein, do cardio if you're overweight, or if you want muscle tone—perform core exercises every-day along with dumbbell training. There are also many types of skin pore cleanses that you can begin performing to help get rid of acne (adult acne is not uncommon).

For ladies, a bit of weight training is more likely to help you lose pounds than gain muscle (muscle tone is very hard to gain, but weight training is still very good for shedding pounds and appearing toned).

As for losing weight, I can save you hundreds of dollars on books and dieting resources by reminding you of one simple fact: when you are burning more calories than you are consuming, you WILL lose weight. Increase exercise, decrease macaroni and cheese, and you WILL fit into that swimsuit or trunks.

In addition to all of these factors, consider your style and grooming; cologne, colors, fashion sense, long hair versus short hair, etc. Don't think too hard about these things, maintain true to yourself, but avoid any major mistakes—like rocking a mullet or dressing like your mom is sending you to church. If you're a guy with a bald-spot, you may want to consider shaving it all off and sporting a manly goatee.

Sometimes it's best to ask a fashion and appearance savvy friend for help.

However, one thing to keep in mind: do not overthink physical appearance! The last thing you want is to adopt some type of body dysmorphic disorder, which as I've discussed earlier is a neurotic obsession with perceived flaws.

I've seen many times men and women alike fall back to excess worrying about not being "pretty enough" or not being "studly / tall enough"; and blaming these factors for their inability to find a boy/girlfriend.

The truth is that these factors matter a lot less than what society may have convinced you to think. In real life, among adults, chemistry and personality is the main factor; and if you're at least giving your appearance and body some amount of effort, then you have as best a chance as anybody.

What to Do Next

Welcome to the often awkward world of dealing with what to do AFTER the ice is broken. The love shy of the world tend to get caught in a kind of abyss-zone, where they have broken the ice with a lovely gentleman or lady, only to start feeling the familiar throes of:

-       Insecurity
-       Running out of things to say
-       Unexpected nervousness

- Bailing out of the conversation too soon
- Not feeling any kind of rapport, and then getting frustrated
- Feeling clueless about how to take things to the next level
- Not leaving with any type of contact information

I like to call these common unfortunate events the **awkwardness spiral of doom**. The conversation may be treading along, but you're stuck in a kind of loop where it doesn't "go" anywhere.

The reason this exists, to greatly simplify things, relates to the tendencies I outlined a few pages ago in chapter one. To recap: a lack of social skills, too high expectations, too low expectations, and intimidation. Furthermore, recall the potential solutions to these habits that I listed a moment ago.

If you're someone who feels chronically awkward around the opposite sex (or same sex, if that's your persuasion), you may have read my advice up until now, and thought "Wow, great ideas!" and then realized that most likely even after internalizing some of what I am saying—you're still the performing the same bad habits.

For this reason, I'm now going to talk about some of the very steps to keep a conversation afloat after the ice is broken, plus some habits to AVOID doing. Keep the previous pointers in mind, especially as your overall philosophy, but the actionable steps below are the next important part of the equation.

- **Avoid the Following Topics:** The weather, sports, politics, peculiar hobbies, business, anything that can fizzle out easily, or anything awkward like exes. The reason is because the wrong conversation will not lead you any closer to what both of you probably desire, which is getting to know one another on a more intimate level. Talking about next week's heat-spell and the lack of rain will create no opportunities for this. Further, **never** talk about your emotional baggage or life problems, including exes. This send all of the wrong messages very early on.

•   **Instead, try this:** Ask him or her personal questions, and appear interested. That immediately makes your partner feel relevant and happy. Share details about yourself, but don't spill all the beans too fast. Ask open ended questions related to ideas and concepts, and what the person enjoys or likes about certain things, e.g.: ("What do you like so much about classic movies?" "What is it that attracted you to this type of place?"). This connects you on an emotional instead of a logical level by engaging a person's imagination.

•   **You don't need to accumulate facts**. Conversing in this way is not a fact-finding mission, and achieving X number of details about a person won't bring you any closer to him or her on an intimate level. In fact, **the more mystery you maintain, the better**.

•   **Also try talking about situational occurrences**. There's no easier way to bond with somebody than to allow something in the moment to bring you together. So if you see something interesting happening a few feet away, talk about it.

• **Provide a way out:** You never want to corner somebody. This is a big mistake. It's why so often people get offended by what they interpret as being "hit on". This has a lot to do with body language (see next chapter), but it also involves not understanding when to take a break. Very often it's better to talk to somebody, leave, and re-engage multiple times. If you just stand there talking long past the point of comfort, or if you "persist" and continue to try and eat up all of his or her time— you'll be creating a tense, uncomfortable situation.

• **Stay in touch:** The more explicit dating coaches like to call this "closing", which is a self-centered term that I don't use. The point, however, is that you can't really date somebody if you don't have a way to see or reach them again. Phone numbers are appropriate, as is any other way to stay in touch, including making future plans together on the spot. Whatever the case is, something needs to be done or else you're just spinning your wheels. I'll talk more about this later.

I Don't Know What to Talk About

Since this is easily the number one "shy person problem", I felt it deserved some special attention.

There is no doubt that conversation can be a sensitive area. The dreaded "awkward pause" is not enjoyed by anyone, and is usually followed by a "nice to meet you", walking away, and banging your head against the wall in the nearest bathroom stall.

There are a couple of pointers that may fix this problem for you:

- **Take Pressure Off**

Famously, it's very hard to be funny when you're "trying" to be funny. Likewise, trying to create the perfect conversation often backfires. Most enjoyable things in life happen from a "flow state". If you walk into any conversation hoping to make everybody laugh and obtain love and affection, you'll be perceived as awkward at best and clingy at worst.

- **Spontaneity is Good**

People are less judgmental of spontaneity than you may think. If a conversation is beginning to reach a lull, there's no shame in being "random". You may open a new subject with "That reminds me of..." pivoting into a new thread concerning whatever impulsive idea just came to your mind.

As long as you show some enthusiasm about what you're talking about, and you avoid negative subjects or some of the do-not-talk-about or boring subjects I mentioned before (the weather, emotional baggage, etc) then it's safe to be imaginative.

If the person you're talking to rejects you because of you are expressing your personality, understand that you'd never be compatible anyway. The best thing you can show somebody who you've just met is the "real you". Usually this is best reflected by whatever comes out of that crazy old head of yours.

- ### It Goes Both Ways

It's good to keep in mind is that your partner is just as worried about running out of conversational steam. Sympathetically try to help them out if they're hitting a lot of stumbling points, and if they feel embarrassed because of a sudden lull that they caused, be caring and let them know it's OK.

- ### Offer to Do an Activity

There's a lot less pressure to talk when two people are engaged in something. This could be walking off to get a drink or going across the street to a museum, coffee shop, or any other excuse to go do something besides stand around and "just talk".

Help, I've Been Rejected!

"Breaking the ice" sometimes leads to the ice breaking YOU. Nobody likes to feel rejected, especially a single person who is perusing the possibilities of romantic connections. Rejections can hurt the ego and make a person question his or her worth.

A rejection may occur in different ways. A person you're trying to talk to will, in an impromptu way, walk away or excuse him/herself. Or, somebody will flat out tell you, "I have a boy/girlfriend. No thanks."

The latter can be very frustrating, because it can occur when you simply thought you were being friendly, and it's hard to be dismissed so blatantly.

Rejection is inevitable. There are a few important ideas to keep in mind to stop feeling so bad when you feel you've been dismissed:

a.   Rejection is probably in your head.

Be careful to not become "that person" who interprets the natural ebbs and flows of conversations to be rejection. If you start seeing rejection everywhere, you will develop an unhealthy psychological complex.

Most of the time, if somebody ends a conversation or gets distracted by something else, that person was not even thinking about you, and it had nothing to do with you. It's very easy to begin misinterpreting every social nuance as a negative sign against you. Be careful.

b.   It's not you, it's them.

Sometimes rejections occur when a person you're talking to, who perhaps you felt a connection to, is suddenly overcome by their own sense of shyness. Afraid to come across wrong, they decide it's better to just bail.

Of course, this is a silly idea on their part, but for somebody with social anxiety it can take a lot of effort to maintain a dialogue with a stranger. Many times people will bail on an interaction before giving it a chance to develop, and they will be upset at themselves after.

Other times, people have entirely different issues. Maybe your large forearms and beard are intimidating her because she has an ex-boyfriend who used to mistreat her and brandished the same beard, so now she's judging you for it. There's almost no way of understanding people's eccentricities.

      c.   They're not really rejecting you.

I'm not suggesting "no means yes", but you'd be surprised how often people will seem to brush you off, only to want to talk to you later under different circumstances. Countless times in the dreaded nightclub scene I'd approach a girl, have her abruptly turn away from me— only to come back to me later in the evening and say "Hey, it's YOU again. Hi."

      d.   You came on too strong.

If you appear to be overtly hitting on someone, you'll more likely get the "I have a girl/boyfriend" talk, or they will innocuously toss reference to their SO at an opportune time.

This doesn't always mean they're even taken, but they're trying to diffuse the situation because they feel uncomfortable. It does, however, mean you came on too strong, too quickly. It means you need to dial down the immediate sexual body language and tone, and focus on some normal dialogue and rapport building first.

Note: if someone is feeling very "available" at that moment, they may respond quite well to said sexual body language and tone. The fact that some people may reject you based on this does not mean it's wrong to do it.

      e.   They just don't like you.

Finally, there are times your attempt at meeting people will be thwarted by the fact that you simply don't align. The thing about humans is that we are a diverse lot, and it's impossible for everybody to always mesh. There are times people will inexplicably not enjoy your company. When this happens, it's not something to fret or obsess over. Instead, go look for the people who do enjoy your company. You are not a god and cannot change your differences.

Chapter Summary

You don't need a perfect approach to meet somebody whom you might be interested in romantically. Finding a date doesn't have to be a very hard or complex process. The key point is to find situations where you have a commonality with the people around you; from groups and clubs, to events and mixers. As you look and feel your best, you increase your chances of obtaining really good chemistry with a special stranger you get lucky enough to meet.

Meanwhile, it takes a level of courage to get oneself out and mingling, especially if shyness is a serious factor. By keeping in mind the social pointers, and understanding the nature of the things you may fear the most—like rejection—it's possible to approach social situations with greater ease. Most of all, however, remember that socializing in this way is a skill-set, as is the very act of meeting people. The more that you do it, the easier it becomes—until you are a full-fledged social butterfly.

HEY! Are you skimming these pages? Slow down a sec, hot-rod.

Hi, nice to meet you. I'm Cyrus, the guy who wrote this thing. That's me below:

Before we continue, I just wanted to ask you to consider joining the Developed Life newsletter.

By signing up, I'll send you a free copy of "**The 10 Success Techniques to Master Your Life**", which is an important supplement to this book. You'll also receive weekly tips about leading a great lifestyle.

In addition, you get access to new books by myself or other authors, with notices when they are available for free or at .99 cents.

Plus, I'm available for FREE life coaching and consultation with ANY problem you have. Why? Because I clearly have too much time on my hands!

To sign up, just head to www.developedlife.com/subscribe and then punch the big "Subscribe" button. I'll see you soon!

Chapter Three – Flirting and Body Language

In this chapter we are going to learn about the factor that separates successful dates from non-successful dates; namely non-verbal communication and creating a romantic (or sexual) dynamic. In other words, when two people go crazy about each other—I'd consider that a VERY successful match.

To understand this topic better, here are some important pointers to start off with:

• Flirting is not an easy subject to accurately define. However, my best effort is as follows: it's the existence of a romantic or sexual subtext to a normal interaction.

• As a subtext, 90% of it occurs non-verbally. This means things like eye contact, the position of your body, and the tone (not the words) of your voice.

• Tone of conversation also greatly impacts whether the context is flirting or not. In general, the more playful it is, the more likely that you are either flirting, or the conversation will turn into flirting.

Are You Flirting Enough?

In the world of dating and relationships, I think a major reason that people stay single or lack options is because they a.) do not know how to flirt, and b.) they are not doing it often enough.

In popular culture, there is a nefarious term, the "friend zone". This is reserved for people who desired a romantic relationship of some type (whether committed, or non-committed), and yet are stuck feeling unsatisfied because they ended up as "just friends".

Why does this happen? The friend-zone enabler may say, "there was no chemistry." This is true, but what he or she meant is that there was no sense of sexual tension or flirtatiousness.

This usually needs to be established from day one. For some reason, the more time is spent without flirting, the harder it is to start doing it. Although it's not impossible to end up going out with, or even marrying, a long-time friend—these are usually special circumstances. Creating sexual communication with somebody it has not already been established with can be daunting. Both parties must want it equally enough to not feel awkward about it.

Therefore, it's a good idea to keep some of the pointers in mind in this chapter, especially when you first meet someone. That is, the initial conversation. Obviously, flirting doesn't happen if there's no "chemistry"—that is, unseen variables that determine how well two people get along. However, in the event that there IS chemistry—NOT flirting would be a great shame! If there's an opportunity to flirt, you MUST take it!

Should I Be a Flirt? Body Language Attraction Cues

A common hang-up is people are clueless about when to act like a flirt and express their attraction. This is why it's important to memorize the many cues that relate to both interest, and disinterest—and to get a grasp on them. These tips relate to both conscious body posturing that you can use to make a person feel attracted to you, as well as the less conscious signs that a sleek observer can detect in-order to understand if their date—or a mysterious stranger—is turned on or not.

One of the most common body language topics you may hear is that, for men, it's important to appear "dominant". These ideas probably stem from a series of experiments that researchers Sadalla, Kenrick and Vershure carried out in the 1980s to identify dominant male traits and their relation to sexual attraction[2].

The study found that men who had an upright bearing, shoulders thrown back, and who moved in a way that evoked "freedom" (being relaxed and uncaring about others around them) were considered more dominant in an evolutionary sense, and it corresponded to female

---

[2]http://psycnet.apa.org/index.cfm?fa=buy.optionToBuy&id=1987-21883-001

attraction. Studies, however, have also shown that while such traits, although attractive, do not necessarily correspond to other traits considered important for mate selection; such as a sense of empathy or compassion.

I think it's safe to assume from these studies that good posture and a sense of confidence as one walks can make a big impact on the first impressions that women have of men, and it may create that initial spark of attraction that you want. However, it's far from the be-all-end-all factor, as coming across very "dominant" without other traits to speak of could actually make a man seem more like a jerk than anything else.

As for attractive body language among women; researchers found far less emphasis on posturing, and certainly "dominance" holds no relevance. However, visual interest and cues are used by women to show their availability, which in return draws men toward them.

Such availability cues can be implemented by both sexes. The following signals indicate somebody is open to be approached:

- Uncrossed arms
- Uncrossed legs
- Smiling
- Standing with feet and body placed in your direction.
- Eye contact with you
- Wandering eyes (looking at different people and unoccupied)

By contrast, closed arms, crossed legs, seriousness and focus on another person are all indicators that such a person is not going to respond well to your advance. If you are worried about whether or not your approach will be successful, consider these external cues to save yourself a lot of time and stress. In other words, don't bother with people unreceptive to conversation.

Finally among both sexes, sitting together and enjoying physical contact is always one of the main signs that the dynamic is fast becoming sexual. Cuddling, touching, and this type of light intimacy is almost always an invitation by one or both parties to take things a little bit to the next level (ie kissing, making out).

Women Showing Interest to Men

For men, how can you tell specifically when a woman is interested?

Often the first sign is if they've provided a sense of space and accommodation to you. A woman who carries a shopping bag or purse will unconsciously use it as a barrier to prevent unwanted approaches. If you're at a party and you are talking to a woman, and she keeps a bag or any other object placed between you and her, it's a clear signal that she does not prefer your company.

Another body signal are feet. According to researchers like Professor Geoff Beattie, a leading psychologist in Britain, the feet hold many clues to a woman's interest in a man[3]. For instance, if a woman sways her feet back and forth or coyly hides them from a man she is talking to; it likely indicates interest. According to Beattie, one of the most powerful signals is if a woman's feet are moving simultaneous to her laughter.

---

[3] http://www.telegraph.co.uk/science/science-news/6709373/How-to-tell-if-a-woman-fancies-you-look-at-her-feet.html

The more common indicators of a woman's interest (that most of us are familiar with) are still important to remember. Any type of emotional spike like blushing, giggling or appealing hyper and excited are great signals of chemistry. Another common indicator that sometimes men miss is proximity. If a woman is standing in-front of you as she speaks, focusing her attention entirely on you, it almost guarantees that she's attracted to you (and that the two of you are "flirting").

It has also been widely recognized that when a woman unconsciously touches her extremities, it indicates she is attracted. The famous cue is when a woman touches her hair. Other signs include touching of the collarbone, sides of the neck, or lips.

Finally, pay attention to eye-contact. This applies to both sexes, but if there's a single non-verbal cue most distinctly related to a romantic or sexual undertone, it's how two people look at each other. Mutual direct eye contact and focus during a conversation is one of the best ways to express a subtle but noticeable attraction. If somebody is disinterested, they will avert their gaze or become distracted easily.

Often two people can be talking about something completely mundane, while staring intently into each other's eyes. Then, sure enough after a few moments, they are passionately kissing. It's quite magical when that happens.

Men Showing Interest to Women

As with anybody on this blue sphere, the personalities of men vary between forward and more docile. That being said, the first indication that a man is interested in you is that he's talking to you. Most men will not come outright and express their overt interest; but they will seek to engage in small talk and hope to carefully nudge things toward a romantic context.

A man who's interested will seek to engage some type of physical contact. It could mean briefly touching the side of the arm as he talks, or saying goodbye while contact is made with an area like the arch of your back. This is sometimes a conscious attempt to establish a more physical dynamic.

A man who is interested will obviously make an attempt at reaching out. Rarely will a man make an effort to call or create some type of longer term contact if he is not interested in dating you. However, most men **require** some type of reciprocal confirmation, or else they will assume you are not interested, and they will find someone else.

What this means is that "playing hard to get", as has been taught in Cosmo mags for decades, is almost certainly the wrong move. The majority of women, for whatever reason, make themselves unavailable romantically. Most men, therefore, get into the habit of testing the waters, and quickly moving on if there is no sign of reciprocal interest.

So that means not returning a phone-call, or not showing any flirtatious body language in response to his, will result in being written off as unavailable. Most men are more than willing to go out on a limb and ask you out, or to try and take things to the next level—but few are willing to risk seeming desperate or facing a humiliating rejection by pursuing somebody who seems uninterested.

The Relationship Between Humor and Flirting

"If you can make a girl laugh, you can make her do anything." – Marilyn Monroe

No section on flirting could be complete without mentioning the importance of humor.

As a rule, the more that you make your partner laugh and feel silly, the more bonding that will occur. Some believe this relates to childhood instincts. Or, it's because you are linking positive, happy emotions to your presence. Whatever the case is, no matter how much you may feel like you are a "deep fish" who only enjoys dark, intellectual conversations—it's important to learn how to lighten the mood and make things more goofy, more fun.

Humor on Dates

There are many ways to approach the art of comedy. However, keep in mind that in dating, your job is not to be a comedian. Rather, the idea is to make enjoyable moments together. Humor, above all, is a way for people to bond.

Think about it; it's very hard to bond over boring, inconsequential things. Humor, no matter its form, is the quickest way to determine a person's real personality, while experiencing a lot of fun positive emotions.

And, humor seems to be a lead-in for more romantic or sexual dynamics. Begin a relationship with laughter, and it will communicate a lot of positive things that will likely keep you out of the so-called "friend zone".

Finally, for you gentlemen, I dare you to find a single woman's dating profile online where she doesn't mention "funny" in her list of attributes that she wants in a guy.

The good news is that you don't have to be "born funny" to develop a funny bone. As any comedy professional will tell you, there's a skill involved—and it includes finding your own innate sense of humor and improving on it. The following is a list of most types of humor—which one best suits you?

Dry and Deadpan

Famous among British comedies. The idea is to say something very clever without cracking a smile or appearing affected. Known as a more intelligent style of humor, a deadpan comedian may be very satirical and also sharp. Some people do not mesh well with this style because they cannot tell if the person is actually being funny or not.

Self-Deprecating

This comedy style places the deliverer as the victim of his or her own jokes. The idea behind self-deprecating humor is to lighten the mood and to make a person seem less important. In a social context, it can make the joker appear less intimidating. It's not uncommon in social situations for somebody who's very important (a boss, celebrity, etc) to make self-deprecating jokes to lighten the mood. Excessive self-deprecation, however, can make a person appear insecure.

Teasing and Banter

In relation to flirting, this is a very powerful concept, and a quick way to shift from a regular, boring conversation into something both fun AND flirtatious. Unlike self-deprecation, teasing involves poking mild fun at the other party. Note, I do say "mild"—not mercilessly making fun.

An example of a tease might be: "I swear you're dressed for Christmas" (she's wearing green and red), or "Are you going for the grundge-rock look?" (if he needs a comb). In other words fun, playful, joking around.

Another way to banter is to "roleplay". This involves setting up different roles, and then assuming them, e.x.: "Ok, I am the world's smartest man, ask me anything" (and just BS the answers), or: "I feel a little sick. You can be my nurse / caretaker /" (etc).

This creates fun and playful options to change up the standard, boring conversation. As with any humor style, don't force it—just look for opportunities to insert a few clever teases or banters.

Slapstick and Goofy

As with any humor style, whether or not you can get away with this type of comedy is entirely dependent on your vibe and relationship with your partner. Some people respond very well to the goofy, slapstick style—which, in the context of dating, could involve things like:

- Tackling
- Pushing / shoving
- Tickling
- Picking up and twirling around

- Chasing around the house
- Chasing around the water fountain
- And all other manner of schoolyard behaviors.

Psychologists will tell you that this type of kindergarten behavior almost always indicates a strong attraction; and it may go hand in hand with not only feelings of love and romantic intimacy; but sexual desire, as well.

In other words, if this type of humorous dynamic is created—consider yourselves lucky! It's a very good sign.

Highbrow and Witty

These are jokes that go over the heads of "average" folk. For some people, witty observations are their own special brand of humor. In the context of dating and relationships, some people bond over their highbrow humor that no one else gets. This may include lots of inside jokes and observations that become special, in their own way.

Dirty and Sexual

Finally, don't discount this one. Obviously, it's not everybody's cup of tea—but sometimes the best way to break the ice in a sexual way is to make jokes about it. Some people are easily offended by this, while others thrive on it. As always, it's a matter of the individuals involved.

What Humor Style is Right for the Two of You?

Figuring out how two people click in a humorous way is as varied as there are pairs of people in the world. However, I do think it's important to find humor on some level—and to establish it as early as possible, such as during a first date.

Your best bet is to first find your own sense of humor, know what it is, and look for a way to express it with your partner. In my experience, if a date does not vibe with your humor, there's a good chance the two of you will have trouble being compatible later on. Therefore, humor is also a way to screen out dates who you might not be able to connect with.

I don't think it's a good idea to ever remain totally serious during a date. I always say the sign a date is working is if he or she is smiling and laughing a lot. Show me two people who are stone cold serious the whole time, and I'll show you a date that is probably going nowhere fast.

The trouble with this concept is that sometimes being funny can feel like going on a limb and exposing oneself to judgment. I notice many people (especially we shy types) are afraid to express our humorous sides, namely because it's like opening a crack in the wall we put around ourselves—where people then get to peer inside and see our true personalities.

This is why I notice among the introverted and shy, funniness is sometimes followed by apologies; "I'm sorry, I'm being weird" or "I'm such a dork sometimes."

It's very unhealthy to express your funny self and then feel any type of shame for it. **The truth is, the more comfortable a person is with themselves, the more their "weird" sense of humor will come out**. I honestly believe the people who are the most serious act that way as a cover, as they are afraid to express the vulnerabilities that are exposed through humor.

When we are children, we tend to express our humorous sides a lot (sometimes mercilessly so), and this is because we have not yet developed that shell of the ego around ourselves. It's only when we become self-conscious of how others think of us that we begin to censor how it is that we express ourselves.

This self-censorship needs to be lessened when we date, especially. You don't want people to get to know the wall of socially contrived behaviors you've set around yourself; you want a person to understand the REAL you. And, humor can be a gateway to do that.

Without establishing humor early on, you run the risk of what I call…

Negative Relationship Patterning

Firstly, this is not a psychological term nor an NLP term that I am familiar with. It's an idea that I've thought of, based on a lot of observation and first-hand experience. Personally, I feel this is one of the most important concepts to learn when dating and trying to develop any type of relationship.

As a man, I began observing my relationships with my female friends. Among my friends, some are women I used to date, some I've never dated, and some of them I seem to have ongoing flirtations with. All of them I can thankfully say are good friends, regardless of our romantic or non-romantic statuses. However, I began wondering about what separates the context of attraction or sexuality from something that feels strictly plutonic.

As of writing this book, I'm in my late twenties. When I was in my early twenties, I was still in an emotional development stage of my life. As thus, I was often afraid to express myself. As I've gotten older, I am no longer very self-conscious, and so I tend to "let loose" a lot more, to the point where I do things previously unthinkable when I was younger—like perform standup comedy out here in Los Angeles.

Not surprisingly, I've noticed that most, if not all, of my female friends from this earlier point in my life are very plutonic by nature. Even close friends are much more "sisterly". I have no problems with this, and I appreciate my relationships with them, but there's a deep contrast to female friends I make today; who I still have close friendships with, but who also maintain flirtatious behavior; a sexually charged subtext.

With the women I meet now, even those whom I become "just friends" with, the idea of those relationships switching to a dating context—intimacy, sex, etc—is not far-fetched, at all—and it actually happens without it being too big of a deal. By contrast, all my very plutonic female friends are essentially far beyond that point. Any attempt to initiate a flirtatious element to my relationships with them would never work, and would endanger those friendships.

Recently I was on Facebook, late night chatting to female friend "A" and feeling very censored, while also talking to female friend "B" about various sexy things. I started to ask myself—what is the difference? How come

55

with one friend, the possibility of her becoming a romantic partner is completely absent, yet with the other friend—it would seem totally normal if it happened?

The answer is that when I used to meet women when I felt very self-censored, I immediately established **negative relationship patterns**. From the moment I met them, there was no flirtatious element present. And so, right from that first meeting I created a **pattern** that we'd subconsciously play along with. That behavioral pattern became a blueprint for the length of the relationship, indefinitely. As more time progresses, changing that blueprint becomes harder and harder to break out of.

By contrast, setting a **flirtatious** behavioral pattern tends to keep the "door open", so to speak. This can be as simple as being a bit goofy at the beginning, telling a dirty joke, engaging in some physical contact, or just setting a proper vibe; whether it's romantic, sexual, or anything else that is related to attraction.

This pattern will last throughout a friendship. And, if it's not established early, it means the difference between having a lot of dates lined up and potential partners, to finding your love life completely absent.

Obviously, this applies to both men and women. In my own life, I've known women who made a point to become my friend while setting a pattern early on that they were not attracted to me (a complete lack of flirtatious behavior or positive body language). Then, later she would confess that she "liked" me (apparently I was supposed to be some kind of psychic guru to figure it out). Although it was not their intention, many people—especially the shy types—avoid signs of interest or flirtatious behavior because they choose to "play it safe" instead; for the same reasons listed above, namely self-censorship and a fear of showing vulnerabilities.

So stay very mindful of the patterns that you develop with people. Understand that the first time you meet someone—or the first date—is going to set the tone for a long time to come. If you act very restricted around someone, you may find that your relationship will feel restricted forever afterward with that person.

Chapter Summary and the Big Point

So what is the main lesson here? The answer is to not play it safe, and to instead *flirt*. If you're interested in somebody, it's better to be friends with a side of flirting than to be forever locked into the frame of being plutonic. Furthermore, it's better to go on a date and risk a bit of humorous teasing, self-expression, and even overt sexual interest than it is to self-censor and be worried about rejection. A date requires this type of "chemistry" for it to grow into something more.

Flirting is most likely to occur when you let your guard down, relax, and enjoy yourself. And one of the best ways to do this is to practice humor. It's hard to pierce an emotional barrier when there is no humor involved; and without defenses being down, it's very hard to signal you are attracted. A date is not successful if both parties are afraid of expressing themselves and feeling self-conscious and insecure. It's your job to prevent these feelings from sabotaging you.

Chapter Four – On Dating Logistics

In this chapter we are going to talk about both dating ideas, and the often difficult topic of asking a person out or initiating something romantic. Truly we are delving into a realm where awkwardness lurks at every corner; and where we shy people need immediate help. Tread forward carefully!

Ignore Most Conventional Ideas

Dating doesn't really exist. In real life, there are gradients to relationships. We go from strictly plutonic acquaintances, to best friends who perhaps love each other but without any type of romantic energy, on to sexually charged relationships where two people cannot be alone together without ripping each other's clothes off.

And this gradient varies. Human relationships vary. Therefore, it's very hard to declare when you are "dating".

Generally the term is used when two people are sleeping together and not seeing anyone else—then they are in a form of relationship, and the colloquial term for it is "dating". However, on the same note, sometimes sex isn't involved. Dating may occur in a totally celibate way, if celibacy is something both parties desire.

Furthermore, dating may occur among multiple people at the same time. In fact, in bigger cities this is practically the standard. Lines between sexual or romantic partner and "friend" are often blurred, and multiple "dating partners" at once is becoming less of a big deal. In popular culture, we may call these situations "friends with benefits". However, in truth, even this term is limiting and not very accurate to express the range of emotions that can be felt amidst the human experience.

The point, however, is that among all of these gradients and variables, nothing becomes official because two people went on a "date". There is no magical activity that creates these dynamics—short of petting, hugging, kissing, or sex. Going to a coffee shop together or watching a movie won't initiate these dynamics.

And, you can go on a hundred dates with a hundred different people and experience no kind of physical intimacy, and not even a Facebook friend add. Dating, in this sense, can be very impersonal. And, people often get a soured impression of the whole process. You may hear people talk about how hard dating is, and it's no wonder—it can be very awkward when two people whom barely know each other get together with preset expectations that something romantic could / should happen, before either person feels any level of rapport within the stranger's presence.

If there's a single destroyer of a date, it's these expectations. Many times, the expectations are cultural, too. Dating becomes a ceremonial thing, where hanging out at a coffee shop is supposed to indicate some first step on a path toward a relationship and finally pushing a baby stroller. But nothing could be further from the truth. In reality, spending time with someone has nothing to do with the activity itself or any type of ceremonial bullshit.

What if I told you that people fall in love in totally unexpected situations?

I know a guy who, one evening, started making out with a girl who worked at a fruit juice bar. They'd been non-verbally flirting for weeks, staring at each other as he'd order his smoothie. Finally, they started just *kissing* while she was on her shift. They just leaned over the customer counter when no one was around and went at it. Obviously the next day, she was sleeping in his bed. Today I think they're engaged.

Did he have to go through the routine of asking her out, taking her to dinner, followed by a movie? No. In fact, if he did those things, maybe they would have never worked out like they did in that spontaneous, "magical" way.

What Does This Mean For You?

It means that you need to reevaluate your dating strategy. If society and tradition has told you that it looks something like:

- Find someone you like
- Ask out (if you're a boy) or wait to be asked out (if you're a girl)

- Chew food in front of each other for a while.
- Awkwardly hug at the end of the night.
- Hope for a call back.

Then you're probably quite mistaken. Consider the following "dating" strategy instead:

- Find someone you like and you've determined you want to "date".
- Look for ways to spend more time with that person.
- Seek to talk and build rapport in whatever way you desire, whether it's chatting in person, on the phone, on Skype—however you want, it doesn't matter.
- Introduce a flirtatious pattern of behavior to show interest, and if there's chemistry, help steer toward some type of physically intimate contact to establish the dating dynamic.
- Alternatively, maintain a cheerful friendship if the romantic intent led nowhere, or otherwise bid farewell if there was simply no chemistry.

You'll always begin as an acquaintance / friend. The turning point is, without a doubt, that moment when lips lock and things change from "hanging out" to something intimate.

The tragic element to the mating game is how so often people will meet, express mutual interest, and desire something to go further—yet BOTH parties fail to "get it" and so they get stuck in one gear. They could meet for a drink, hang out at a coffee shop and discuss whatever nonsense is on the news. Meanwhile, they are both fantasizing in their minds about what their lips feel like on each other, and yet neither do anything to satisfy that desire. They just stare at each other, awkwardly hug, and then return to their respective apartments (and pet cats), feeling lonely and wondering why their love lives are so inactive.

It really is quite sad because it's inner fear and limiting beliefs that are blocking the chance for progress to happen. Consistently, it happens because each party is hesitant to show *signs of attraction*. They keep their body language closed, they avoid humor, banter and teasing (see previous chapter), and they talk about boring, uninteresting topics.

In other words, they are going through the motions of a "date" without practicing the specific social skills needed for a date to actually progress in the way it's supposed to. This is how dates "fail".

So, How Do I Ask That Cutie Out?

If we are getting away from the traditional dating dynamic, where does that leave us as we deal with the age old dilemma of how to pop the infamous question?

The reason I used to have much difficulty in my teens with the concept of dating and relationships was because I did NOT like "asking someone out". To me, it felt awkward and stilted. "So, uhh, do you wanna go out sometime?" were the 7 (8, counting the 'uhh''s) words of doom in my mind, usually followed by a gut-wrenching rejection; something to the effect of: "Umm, thanks, but I'm waxing my eyebrows that night."

As humans are extremely pattern-oriented, we have learned to identify the pattern of being asked out on dates, which is synonymous with being pressured into a relationship / dating dynamic; often by somebody who is more infatuated with us than we are of them. As a result, it's no wonder asking somebody out can be perilous.

As an alternative to this same routine, here are some things to consider instead:

-        Focus, firstly, on establishing a connection. The more of a connection you have, the more natural "asking out" becomes. And, obviously, if the two of you are flirting, that's a big bonus.

-        What this means is look for every opportunity to talk to the person and establish your relationship to him or her. Facebook, phone, Skype, after class, studying in the library—whatever and wherever.

-        Practice some level of humor as we discussed in the last chapter. The more you can keep that person smiling, the more he or she will want to be around you – GUARANTEED!

-        After that person already enjoys your company and it's obvious, start inviting them to things with you. These can be your "dates".

-        At this point, spending time with that person will NOT feel awkward, forced or high-pressure. This is because you've already established that relationship.

I am not saying it's impossible to begin "dating" someone by asking them out before getting to know them. For instance, sometimes "blind dates" work out really well, because there is that established context that you're on a "date" and therefore some spark of romance is expected (and allowed) to happen.

Many will argue that the advantage of the "old fashioned" way is that it does create that all-powerful expectation, which means you are less likely to end up in a nebulous, "friendship" zone. This is a valid argument, and something to take into consideration.

If you are shy, however, those blind-dates can be the worst. While I advocate going outside the comfort zone always, sometimes the pressure and judgment felt in these situations can be just too much to handle.

When two people don't know each other very well, they default to judgments. A judgment is a snap decision made about something using minimal resources and facts. We use judgments for the purposes of filtering information and guarding ourselves. For instance, if we see an older guy in a van with tinted windows pull up to a park with children playing, and he's wearing a trench-coat, odds are we'll call the police—even if he's totally innocent.

What I've noticed on dates is that before there's a prior established relationship, the judgments come in spades. How you're dressed, minor behavioral characteristics, physical flaws, and a lot more become defining criteria.

So while these types of blind dates can work—and you may meet your future significant other this way, I feel it's wiser (and easier) to work within your social circle, finding people through the groups and activities I listed in chapter two, and then slowly building those relationships, instead of stacking too many expectations on at once, and then collapsing the whole process as a result.

Making the Date Work, and Making a Move

What I am not going to do is start going on and on about "first date ideas". A lot of books do this, and I find it annoying. The reason it's silly to focus on this is because the location you go to doesn't matter. It could be tango dancing or a grocery store to buy deodorant. What matters is if there's chemistry or not.

One steadfast rule to keep in mind, however, is to avoid two types of activities: **low-interaction dates** and **forced-interaction dates**.

The former, the low interaction date, is best encapsulated by going to a movie. While sitting in a dark movie theater might be a great excuse to make-out, you probably don't know this person well enough for this strategy to work just yet (but if it does work, kudos, my friend). Otherwise, the theater is a bad environment because your focus is spent on the movie and not your *date*. Since you can't converse in the theater, it becomes a low-interaction activity and it will not move the two of you anywhere near the right direction.

(Watching a movie at your place, cuddling on a couch is—however—an entirely different matter.)

The latter no-no is when an interaction is *forced*. The best example of this is the infamous "dinner date". It's fine to go to dinner with someone *after you already know them very well*, but trying to establish chemistry this way is a bad idea. There's nothing that screams "awkward" quite like staring at each other chew and trying to think of the next thing to say.

The ideal activity involves something that diverts attention from each other, while promoting interaction. So that could be virtually anything: hiking, shopping, dancing, playing arcade games—whatever.

Just remember, the "date" is not as important as building a connection, which you can do anywhere—not just during the sacred "date" ritual. It could be on the phone or at an office vending machine; it doesn't take a special situation to establish a romantic dynamic.

What About All the Dating Cliches?

There are a lot of "dating clichés" floating around modern society. This ranges from the traditional; like the man picking the woman up at home and paying the bill, to the less-traditional societal conditioning—that there's pressure to sleep with him or her after the second or third date.

As a rule of thumb: ignore societal conditioning. Unless you're dating the preacher's daughter in a small town, it's unlikely to be considered vital to play by the old rules, as most people exist in a modern paradigm. As for sex by date two, this is also arbitrary. While it's important to establish a physical "more than friends" dynamic, this can be done through kissing and light intimacy—sex doesn't have to happen immediately if you don't want it to.

This is not to say traditions and rules still don't apply. As we'll discuss momentarily, there's still a lot of old-time beliefs in relation to courtship, such as how it's the man's responsibility to make a first move or otherwise lead the interaction. This type of social conditioning is not so easy to shake off, and unfortunately we still have to play within that framework sometimes, at least until our culture begins to change.

About Making the First Move

First of all, congratulations for making it this far in this book. People who are not very serious are statistically most likely to have shelved it by now. So, it looks like you're in it for the long haul.

If, however, you haven't been paying full attention so far (yes, Mr. / Ms. Skimmer, I'm looking at *you*), then I want you to now put aside that itchy trigger-finger page-turner, and start reading closely—because 90% of dating related problems are related to this one issue: it's where, I have no doubt the most amount of people experience some level of pain and difficulty.

At some point, to cross the threshold of "friends" into "romantic partner", **a move must be made**. In general, **this takes the form of a kiss**. Sex could certainly be part of this equation, as well—however, sex rarely begins without kissing first.

I want to make something clear: **everyone is afraid of making the move**. There's nobody walking this green earth who isn't in some small way intimidated by this. I've seen businessmen who can close multi-million dollar deals and destroy enemies in court-rooms feel paralyzed by the idea of initiating a first kiss. Likewise, it scares most women—and they default to societal expectations that it's the men who must take charge of this area (and as a result, nothing ever happens).

Why are people scared of this? The answer is related to any intense emotional episode—a fear of personal imbalance. As psychologist John Montgomery writes in *The Embodied Mind*, such episodes of intense fear represent a drive to re-enter a state of homeostasis (happiness, comfort, security), where there is no pressing survival-related threat[4]. Obviously jumping out of an airplane can trigger this feeling, as logically it would seem a deathly move—but why kissing?

Some evolutionary biologists theorize that it's related to the great importance placed on the mating game by our caveman ancestors, and that choosing the wrong mate could have deadly consequences. For instance, a caveman caught making the move on a tribe leader's girl would promptly get his head crushed by a large rock.

This is a worthy theory, and I think it holds merit, but my view is that it relates more to the ambiguous world of human psychology. Inside each of us is a boiling cauldron of paranoia, projections, and insecurities, and one thing most of us fear is rejection and negative emotions. I still remember negative, awkward moments of rejection that occurred many years ago, and these are not pleasant memories. Naturally, we fear similar episodes will occur again. In addition, we may project a lot of value on an interaction, and our insecurities manifest as a deep fear of loss—that we'll screw up our precious date and be given an ugly reminder of our own inadequacies.

In other words, a very benign act is given a great deal of importance based on what are usually abstract concepts of loss, rejection, happiness, and lack of happiness. The amount of importance that we place on something like this actually hardwires our bodies to react emotionally, as if we were placing our lives in jeopardy. As a result, the homeostasis-seeking response occurs, with all of the signatures of fear and anxiety that rises from our mind and into our physicality; rendering the best of us unable to lean forward and be physically intimate.

---

[4] http://www.psychologytoday.com/blog/the-embodied-mind/201209/emotions-survival-and-disconnection

However, if you do not get over this fear (or "shyness", for lack of a better term) and make the first kiss happen, **you're going to be stuck in first-gear forever**. It's that first act of physical intimacy that completely changes the dynamic between two people. There is no longer confusion or grey-zones in-between friendship and something more. It's absolutely necessary to do this, **and it's best to make that move on the FIRST date, AKA the first time you are spending 1-on-1 time together.**

It should be a three-step process. This applies to BOTH sexes, not just men who are normally supposed to be the ones to lead this forward. Rather, if a woman is interested she should not hesitate to make a move, too. Here's what you should do:

-       Express some flirtatious signals. This is what I talked about in chapter three. A combination of humor and body language that exhibits your interest.

-       **See if those signals are reciprocated**. If flirting appears two ways and there's mutual interest, **it's an invitation.**

-       Don't wait too long or overthink it. **You don't have to lock lips, it can be a peck**. Wait a few moments, preferably during some type of humorous banter, then say "Hey", lean in and give the peck. You can pause though, because if the reaction is very positive, it would be wise to go in and make it a more 'serious' kiss.

Given that there are still inevitable gender roles in place that persuade the interaction, here are some points to consider:

- Men are usually still expected to make the first move.

- If you're a man, you can give yourself permission to NOT make the move if (and only if) she is showing no signals. I don't think it's a good idea to make a move if there is no indication it's what she wants. If a woman does desire for things to turn physically intimate but she fails to cue him in that she likes him, then it's more her fault. No man that I am aware of is a mind-reader.

- However, as a man, there is NO excuse to not make the move if she is showing signs of interest (flirtatiousness, positive body language, etc). It has to be somebody's responsibility to steer the ship in the proper direction.

- If you want to increase the chances that he will kiss you, try deliberately flirting. Lean close to him, touch his shoulder while you talk, look into his eyes, and create proximity. If he responds with nervousness or does not appear to enjoy the sudden closeness, it likely indicates that he is not interested in you romantically.

- Please show some sympathy if the kiss fails. If the timing was off or otherwise he tried to kiss you in an inappropriate circumstance, understand that he was most likely trying his best and certainly meant no harm by it. It's not necessary to cancel the date unless you truly feel uncomfortable around him.

Logistically, Where Do I Make the Move At?

There's a lot of hang-ups about this topic, too. It should be under the moonlight by a fountain, at your place when you are sitting together, during a hot-air balloon ride; you get the picture.

The truth is that the perfect moment won't really occur. It could be while you're walking and talking, sitting down somewhere randomly, or in a car together.

Personally, I think the trick is to not make it a high-pressure ordeal. A peck on the lips is all it takes to "open the door" for more possibilities, and it should be innocent enough that it's not something that can be a big problem or require some type of awkward rejection process.

If there's anything the "kisser" should be communicating; it's curiosity, and a bit of vulnerability. Making the move does place a person in a vulnerable position emotionally; and it does take a bit of courage to do it; however, it's necessary to explore the potential chemistry that results in going for a kiss. If your partner in some way can understand these sentiments, it makes the process a lot easier.

"Let's Just Be Friends"

The most common "rejection" a person will hear if the "first move" didn't go right (I use quotation marks a lot, don't I? it's because I prefer to approach any generality with a grain of salt) is the "LJBF" talk.

Personally, I think giving someone this talk is a bad idea. Many people, unfortunately, don't know what they want. And so, they may give a person signals, enjoy the flirting, but when things are actually taken to the next level—they get cold feet, and say "No, no, let's not go this route anyway. Let's just be friends, instead".

"Just friends" greatly marginalizes relationships. It also puts a barrier up. Firstly, if you absolutely detest his or her company—you shouldn't be doing one-on-one activities with him or her in the first place. If the LJBF talk is given, it virtually eliminates *any* chance that something will flourish in the future. You've essentially created an impenetrable glass ceiling that will make any future contact with the person seem awkward.

A much better response might be "Let's take things slow, okay? I'm not ready for kissing just yet." This makes the point clear, without marginalizing. Personally, the best "rejection" I ever received from a kiss was when the woman said "You're as crazy as I am, Cyrus". We got a good laugh about it and it didn't hurt the friendship.

If you are on the receiving end of the LJBF talk, in my opinion you have every right to bring that friendship to a halt. It's not fun maintaining a friendship with somebody when there's a glass ceiling in place; especially if you're attracted to that person but they're just not that into you. Provide a lot of distance and stop contacting that person; and definitely don't pursue something that isn't there. If their feelings begin to change, they'll come back to you instead. Otherwise, there are many, many more humans on this sphere that we can meet.

Does this mean you should cut off the date, though?

Here's another awkward conundrum that many people face. If you are having a good time with somebody, you go for a kiss, and you get the LJBF talk, what are you supposed to do then? Walk away and pout about it? Pretend like nothing happened and continue activities as normal?

What I suggest is to embrace the awkwardness, point it out, and end the date. Tell him or her "Okay, I feel very strange now. I think we should call it a night. It was nice spending time with you. I'm heading back to my car now.". You don't have to feel ashamed for doing this. What WOULD be shameful, on the other hand, is forcing yourself to go through the motions of playing miniature golf (or whatever your date activity is) when you're on a completely different emotional page.

Whatever you do, do NOT apologize about going for a kiss! It's natural, it's healthy, it's normal, and it SHOULD be done sooner than later. If you provoke a negative reaction, all you're doing is bringing the nature of your relationship with that person to the surface. The kiss, which is such a powerful tool, almost immediately reveals everything that is normally unseen. So whether they adore you or are disgusted by you, the kiss is going to reveal all.

As an example, one time I went for that kiss with a woman who was giving me virtually no signals that she was interested (I had a couple of drinks, which helped inspire me, I guess). She responded by almost tackling me—in a public venue, at that. Apparently, I had awoken within her a lot of sexual desire for me that she had been trying to hide from the surface. Needless to say, that was a successful date. And, we would not have started dating if I hadn't taken that risk.

The moral is, you won't know until you make the move. Yes, it's a moment of truth, but there is often no better feeling in the world than the first kiss with somebody. It's truly an incredible experience, and when it works right—it's worth all of the tension and difficulty that it sometimes takes to get there.

Moving to the Next Level

While inner-city activities are fun, and it's a way to get to know someone, a question lingers about moving from the dating realm and into more of a relationship.

The hallmark of this involves spending 1-on-1 time with a person to a greater extent; until other dating prospects become less apparent. In other words, it indicates the role in each other's lives has expanded beyond a casual level.

In many cases, it takes a bit of time before people are comfortable enough to do this. In general, some type of intimacy will have already been established first. This type of close, private company will also typically involve an increase of sexual activity, as well—and this is certainly a major component of going from the nebulous dating world into that of a relationship in the more official sense.

Obviously, another tenant is exclusivity. While this is the 21st century, and many people now refrain from exclusive-anything until it's time to tie the knot (or permanently move in together), there are still many couples who do desire this type of arrangement. However, the preferences at this point are entirely up to the couple. I am of the personal opinion that total exclusivity should be saved for marriage and a family, and it's premature to jump into those waters before that time. However, certainly many people, and many couples, would disagree.

As these factors coalesce, it will eventually become fair to say you're in a relationship territory. And if you are happy together, then the "dating" process has ultimately worked for you successfully—congratulations!

Maintaining excitement and those loving feelings in a relationship may be the topic of another book—but for now, just remember that it's OK to take things slow, and keep the pressure off. Something that can interrupt both relationships and dates alike is desiring too much, too fast. Just because you really want to start thinking about baby names after three weeks does not mean your partner is on the same page. Deciding on a person as your life partner is one of the biggest decisions a person can make—so avoid pressuring or moving "too fast".

Chapter Summary

The main point of this chapter is that **you have to make a move if you want a date to work—and to escape friendship territory**. The longer you wait to make something happen, the harder it will be for you to establish such a dynamic.

Furthermore, we shy types have a tendency to fear this process. Both going for a kiss as well as the initial move of asking a person out. These moments can be painfully awkward if not approached the correct way. It's understandable, given that we are putting everything on the line—including our fragile egos.

To make it all less awkward, learn the art of understanding signals of attraction. The key to making a move, and creating a successful date, involves both understanding if you are attracted, and then determining if your partner is, too. If the signals are there, and the body language is unmistakable, then it's much easier to make that jump and go for the kiss.

As for asking him or her out, remember that the idea is to focus on building rapport. A connection can be built anywhere—not just during a date. The less of a connection is already established before you "ask out", the harder it will be and the greater the likelihood of a rejection.

Chapter Five – Limiting Beliefs and Dating Falsehoods

"Everything in the world is about sex. Except for sex; sex is about power" – Oscar Wilde.

In his usual pithy form, Wilde sums up many unhealthy societal views about sex, dating, and the entire courtship and mating process. No other topic on this Earth is more consumed by bad ideas, societal brainwashing, and misconceptions. It is also a major source of insecurity and personal self-esteem related problems. How can we tackle so many issues in one chapter? Well, I will certainly try my best. Let's get started.

When Sex and Dating is About Power Versus Love

Perhaps one of the reasons dating and courtship is a topic people find intimidating is because it's interwoven with ideas about self-worth, sexual identity, and the power associated with sexual desirability. Other people are more stricken by these thoughts than others, but everyone is affected in some way. This ultimately explains everything from chronic loneliness and the involuntarily celibate, to massive divorce rates.

Covetous, jealousy, manipulation, and viewing people as conquests—these are all the vices of the mating game. And, the more that you play in that arena, the more you may find that your love life suffers as a result.

These attitudes are best illustrated in the nightclub or any party centered, social atmosphere filled with strangers. The assumed social roles immediately come to the surface—the women are the targets and the choosers, and the men are the seekers. Women cluster together with their drinks, in their respective social circles. Men from the outside stare at them, wondering how the hell they're supposed to go and talk to them.

And soon, men begin trying their best. They memorize openers and routines off the internet, which are generally fake and uninteresting. Many of them have a dual purpose to try and show off to their buddies—after-all, sexual prowess is a symbol of masculinity. One by one, they approach—and get destroyed. The women put up their "disinterested" body language—arms crossed, purses in-front of them, and they play the Friday night game of shooting torpedoes at would-be suitors.

After a while, one of the ladies finds herself somewhat attracted to one of the men—maybe it's his dark hair, strong cologne and excess confidence. And so, she begins entertaining his attention, and she leaves her group and goes to the bar with him.

Their conversation is not that interesting—it's about her pet cat. The man nods in feigned interest as he sips his Manhattan and listens to her, but secretly he's wishing he had found one of her friends instead of her. Although they're far from ripping each other's clothes off—on the outside, their uninteresting exchange actually looks like he just pulled her from her friends in a stroke of social brilliance, and is now seducing her like a true Don Juan.

What happens next is almost as predictable as clockwork—the other guys in the club start to feel jealous. Because they assume Don Juan is more skilled and with greater sexual prowess than them, they begin harshly criticizing themselves. In the movies, real men go to nightclubs and score one night stands, and each guy watching Don in action is forced to think "How am I so inadequate? What is THAT guy doing that I'm not?"

Among the jealousy mongers, one guy in particular decides he will NOT be fucked with. Don Juan can go to hell, HE is the true alpha male. And so, he buds into their conversation. He hands Don his Jagerbomb and inserts himself in-between the two of them. The woman's now feeling a bit warm and fuzzy thanks to her Cosmopolitan, and her inhibitions have weakened. And so the alpha male's brute grab for attention is temporarily interesting to her, and she entertains his attention long enough to piss Don off; and the squabble that results between Mr. Alpha and Don quickly turns uncomfortable; and she retreats to her friends.

After some harsh words are exchanged, the bouncer detects a fight brewing; and both guys end up kicked out to the curb. The alpha dude dusts himself off, collects his friends, and goes to the next club. Don Juan goes home angry and avoids going to the clubs again for a couple of months. The lady in the story returns home to her three pet cats, curious why she has such bad luck.

If that story sounds familiar to you, it's how the mating process seems to inevitably play out again, and again. If you read between the lines in that story, you'll notice a lot of twisted dynamics, and in a way it's everybody's fault for playing into it. The end result is that very often—nobody wins. While I don't doubt that some people do hookup at nightclubs, in real life (not Hollywood), the only thing most people sleep with at the end of a night on the town are their pillows.

The women, in many ways, enjoy the attention. They like to be seen in crowded venues, and while they may complain about "annoying guys", in truth they enjoy the sense of power that comes with rejecting 90% of their potential suitors. It's the same phenomenon as being addicted to posting selfies—it's a high received from sudden self-approval and attention. It's narcissism made manifest, and it's not healthy.

As for the men, in most situations women becomes synonymous with sport. Men take their sexual abilities VERY seriously, and they continuously judge each other about it. The word "virgin" is used among male circles as the lowest form of insult. And, when you have men's self-esteem and egos on the line, inevitably you get: jealousy, anger, pushy behavior, and all-out fist-fights. And, it's not healthy.

If you think these problems end beyond the bars, you're wrong. The same vices appear again later as men "show off" their girlfriends; getting high from the jealousy others feel. It also manifests when women use sexuality as a method of manipulation; perhaps chatting up an attracted male in-front of her partner as a means to spur jealousy and manipulate him into behavior that she desires.

Some would argue the majority of this behavior is biological. Others say it's sociological, related to gender roles. I might say it's about good old-fashioned emotional immaturity. Nonetheless, perhaps now you can see what Oscar Wilde was talking about. The mating game is rarely as simple as meeting someone and enjoying the chemistry. Instead, so often, all of these vices are interwoven into it.

Some Proposed Solutions

The difficulty with being a shy, introverted type is we may be slightly more sensitive to these negative aspects of the mating game. As a result, it's one of the many reasons we may choose to be alone on a Friday night with some wine, a movie, and (inevitably) a pet cat or dog on our laps.

The best way to fight against the dark side is to make sure you've eliminated the habits from your own life. Naturally, you'll attract a higher standard of people as a result.

Some of this advice is geared toward men, and others toward women—it should be fairly obvious which is which.

- **Don't Treat Women as Conquests, Yes Even the Pretty Ones**

There is a common phenomenon where men like to place women on pedestals; namely for physical appearance factors. I think this condition is exacerbated in the 21st century when youth and beauty are literally worshipped and men are force-fed diets of pornography.

As a man, I find nothing wrong with finding myself stricken by a beautiful woman. In fact, it's an AMAZING feeling—I love it. However, it's NO excuse to prop that person up as something you can show off. This goes back again to that ego-driven lust for power. A man wants to feel powerful, to be able to say he acquired some woman that only exists in every other male's fantasies. There's a lot of obvious reasons this attitude will hurt you—namely, it's reducing human beings to materiality and status.

And, by the way, ladies—you're not exempt from this behavior. I used to go to school with an Abercrombie & Fitch model. Every girl on sorority row wanted him solely for the status that would be associated with dating him. Trust me, he was not as happy about this situation as you may guess. Being reduced to a status symbol is not fun for anybody.

- **Men Who Approach You Are Not Malicious, They Just Want Hugs**

Being a male, I've spent a great deal of time with fellow males, and I can say with some degree of certainty that most of the guys I've been out with on weekends who start approaching women are neither rapists nor do they feel entitled. In reality, they're insecure and really want some type of human interaction.

In my story earlier, I used the analogy of women shooting potential suitors down like torpedoes. Sometimes this is necessary when that one pushy, clingy jerk doesn't get the message. However, if you're perpetually single, you may consider letting your defenses down a little bit.

It's easy to get into the habit of constantly rejecting, constantly exerting your power in the sexual marketplace, but again—it won't cure your inability to find a date. Before you judge the guy for being geeky, creepy, douchebaggy, or any other "y" adjective, try talking to him and see if there isn't some type of chemistry. Often we click surprisingly well even with random people.

And, do keep in mind when a guy approaches a girl, he's sometimes mustering as much courage as he possibly can. He may be a fellow shy type who is completely going outside of his comfort zone. That should be admired at least a little bit, right?

- **Treat Your Sexuality As a Gift, Not a Weapon**

I would say this applies to both boys and girls. Don't allow your sexual charisma to go to your head. As soon as attraction, sex, and dating becomes ego-centric, you're in trouble.

From the woman who's so striking every single man stares at her with desire, to the man whose words are so smooth that few women can resist, a few of us do have these charms. Such abilities do not, however, make you more special than anyone else.

The fact that you can create sexual desire means it should be handled cautiously and with respect. If you attempt to use this ability as a means to siphon value and exert power, you could become a force of darkness instead of good.

I've seen it myself in the murky world of pickup artists and professional seducers; allowing their sense of ethics to take a backseat to finding the next conquest. This is where sex once again becomes about power. Interestingly, those guys who are obsessed with obtaining more notches than their peers often share commonalities of not being very happy; and not finding meaningful relationships. Certainly, the same behavior can manifest in women, as well.

If you find you have the ability to turn others on and be sexually appealing; think about how you can use it to make your future partner happy, not about how you can exploit it to seduce and destroy.

- **People Do Not Represent Their Genders**

There is festering hatred in this world, and a sizable chunk of it is related to gender animosity. I point the finger directly at viscous genderist movements and websites—including both certain "Men's Rights" communities as well as extreme feminist ideologies.

Genderism exists as a result of a predictable behavior pattern: "a boy or girl hurt me, therefore all boys or girls are this way". Get a bunch of people like that in a room together, and they form a club. It's all downhill from there.

Sweeping judgments are easily the lowest form of human consciousness. It spurs everything from racial hatred to religious violence. Never characterize the opposite gender, even as a jest. Never say "All men are this way" or "All women are that way".

Doing so places your love life in permanent jeopardy. It may also hurt all future relationships. Logically, there is no excuse for this type of thinking. The action of one person does not, and never will, reflect some greater trend among people.

- **All People Are Your Brothers and Sisters**

Uh oh, this sounds a little creepy, huh?

Hear me out. Stop sizing people up based on whether you'd date them or not date them. Whether they turn you on or don't turn you on. Or, how badly you want to acquire someone and beat everyone else to be the first to get him or her in the sack.

Competition models of reality are toxic, and sizing people up as objects is doubly toxic. Instead, consider that everyone is your brother or sister at their core. Other humans that you're temporarily sharing this world with.

Seek to put people on the same level playing field as you. A supermodel does not have more status than a cashier. A hot billionaire CEO does not have more status than the guy who takes out your garbage. So, don't make dating decisions based solely on societally identified status—because such an ego-driven box will severely limit you and spread unhealthy outlooks of the world.

(Please reference the exercise back in chapter one—taking people off of pedestals.)

The Dangers of Needing Validation and Approval

One of the patterns of thinking that endangers your love life the most is seeking validation and acceptance. While this is a systemic problem that takes many forms, it expresses in the dating world as neediness, clinginess, and trying to move things forward too fast. An example might be asking someone you've known for two weeks to move in with you. Other examples include any form of stalking or obsession about your partner.

The core of this limiting belief is: "I'm not good enough as I am". If you bring this mentality into dating and relationships, it will cause a lot of problems. For one thing, you'll always be looking for patterns to reinforce this idea. Any type of perceived rejection will be taken to heart, and be a confirmation of inadequacy.

Needy, clingy behavior can kill things before they ever start. Somebody who's emotionally sound will sense there's something "off" about you, and they will not pursue things any further. This mentality breeds emotionally codependent relationships, and people who are not codependent will steer clear of you.

Curing such conditions may be in the realm of psychiatric care. However, you can start by training yourself to be self-accepting. Self-development is truly about letting go of conscious and unconscious negative patterns about yourself. This includes feelings of inadequacy about your physical appearance, speech, social skills, status, worthiness among peers, and so forth.

Unfortunately, in schools emotional intelligence is not taught. How well we accomplish our goals and fulfill our roles in society is of the utmost importance, but how happy and self-accepted we are is not even taken into consideration. It is no wonder that people leave the educational system well-trained in their vocations but emotionally and psychologically vulnerable.

I have no idea how badly affected you might be by these negative ideas, but be mindful about your insecurities. Just remember that the less energy that you give to your perceived flaws, the less power that they have over you.

The Ten Percent Disease

Living in Los Angeles, I've found the "ten percenters" to be very common. This is another odd philosophy that definitely hurts people's love lives.

In the big city, many of us are career-minded. Los Angeles, New York, London—these are places where competition is fierce, and the desire to reach the top is strong enough to blind people with ambition. In much the same way that people strive for the best job, the highest salary, and the most fame—people also competitively seek the best mates.

In many ways, this doesn't make any sense—how can we compete over getting the best partners? This indicates that people are valuable based on a gradient scale that's somehow universal. It neglects the fact that compatibility differs between people. It turns all of our relationships into a status-based pursuit.

The ten percent disease is when a person seeks only what they perceive as the top ten percentile of partners. They will mercilessly weed out candidates who do not fit their standards of being "the best".

These are the ladies who subscribe to the rule of 6's (six pack abs, six figure income and six feet tall), or the men who place great judgments about things like hip ratio, symmetry, boob size, etc.

Their never-ending quest is to find the perfect woman, or "Mr. Right". They would rather live alone and never find a partner than settle for somebody who's "second rate". They place their love lives on the same playing field as their careers and quest to reach the top of the social hierarchy.

And, they are reinforced in this behavior by the media, peers, TV shows, etc.

In actuality, ten percent syndrome is part of the same insatiable materialism that plagues so many and creates endless unhappiness. Not only does it severely limit your dating pool, but it makes you judge people's worth as human beings on meaningless criteria.

When this syndrome is in action, a man or woman will be perpetually single, as going on dates with such a person will be uncomfortable for the other party, because it will always feel like a job interview is taking place. Instead of relaxing and getting to know such a person, the victims (dates) will instead feel like they are in the hot-seat; with no room for error.

Without fail, when decent people run for the hills around ten-percenters, he or she will rationalize it by saying "Oh, that date wasn't good enough for me anyway". The truth, however, is that their crushingly complex standards are limiting their choices to only a small percentage. If they ever do find someone, it was after basing most of their standards on surface level things ("Wow! He's a TV producer") and then they become disappointed when they find out there was no real connection after-all.

And thus, we have massive divorce rates in the United States and many other countries!

Don't be a ten-percenter. It's good to have standards, but there's a difference between having such standards and being a closed-minded pursuer of some pie-in-the-sky perfect mate. Further, if you base your love life as something akin to you professional quest-for-the-best, you will always be sorely disappointed.

Misc. Negative Opinions About Sex and Dating

Now let's look briefly at some further negative beliefs that could be keeping your love life twisted in a knot. Some of these ideas are deep-seeded, and I don't know if you'll recover from them by reading a singly goofy book you found on Amazon. But, they're important concepts to keep in the back of your mind, in case some of these hit home more than others.

"I'm Not Attractive"

I do believe that objectively speaking, a person can be unattractive. If you're obese, it's in your best interest to diet and do what you can within your abilities to get in better shape. If you are filthy, you should bathe more. If your teeth are a mess, it might be time to get a dentist.

You will eventually, however, reach a ceiling when you've done the most that you can do on a physical level. You lost twenty pounds, your fashionista friend helps you dress, and you even wore braces for a year. At this point, the only thing stopping you from being attractive is your personality and attitude.

An attractive personality is anybody who exhibits some level of charm and positivity. This can be as simple as being in a good mood—that's it! Good moods are contagious and people want to be around other people who are feeling happy, because it brings them up, as well. I can't tell you how to be happy. Only you can walk that path with accuracy. But however it is that you do it, you must practice it.

The dark-side to continually telling yourself that you're not attractive ranges from physical personal abuse (anorexic conditions, addiction to plastic surgery) to long-term depression. Don't be caught in such a dark spiral; start believing you're attractive, and watch what happens.

"Sexuality is Sinful"

Religion is no excuse to adopt this belief. The puritanical days are long over. Choosing to be celibate or not is your own path, but don't live a life of shame or regret based on sex. If you choose to have sex, don't do it despite some horrible feeling that you're going to hell.

Negative sexual opinions are not just of the religious kind; but they can also involve feeling shameful of being too easy, or a "slut". In all but extreme cases, these criticisms are not relevant. The reason is because in my experience, the sooner a relationship dynamic switches to sexual, the better.

Whether it's making out and foreplay, or the entire thing—it guarantees you're in a position (no pun intended) to have a real, passionate lover—and not somebody who is caught in some type of awkward in-between zone. Usually the sooner this is established, the better. Relationships that begin passionately tend to stay passionate.

"I'm Too Old"

Whether you're 30, 40, 50, 60 or older—everyone feels this way at different times in their lives. When I turned 17, I freaked out that I was getting old. At 21, I thought it was all over for me (as time goes on, however, I've begun caring less and less. Now I'm approaching 30 and who cares?).

It is true there are less available singles when you're out of the 20s party scene, but it's hardly an excuse that'll keep you trapped as a victim of the "forever alone" meme. There's plenty of opportunities to still meet people, at all ages.

This is harder, I believe, among women. In a looks-centered culture, many women have mini-meltdowns when their 20s ends and their ivory skin and wrinkle-free face starts to show marks of maturity.

Instead of panicking, just think about it this way: relationships built ONLY on physical appearance tend to be shallow at best, and disastrous at worst. Many people, as they age, will attribute their mature looks as a blessing in disguise. Instead of only attracting those obsessed with youth and vanity; they begin filtering higher quality people into their lives.

So, getting older might really be an opportunity for brand-new possibilities.

"I'm the Prize"

This is common advice that gets passed to people as a way to empower them in the dating world, and it's all rubbish.

If you constantly tell yourself "I'm the prize" you'll be entering a selfish state of mind. Yes, you might be a prize, but please enlighten me about what you really offer someone.

Any kind of relationship, including casual dating, is about give-and-take. Never get into the habit of believing that you're an entitlement king / queen. If some element of your behavior is off-putting to dates; consider how you can work on yourself. Do not simply dismiss the negative impressions you make as the *other* person being unworthy of you. This is a rationalization, and boy I've seen this one a lot. Often among people with glaring personality flaws who are afraid to look at what the real issue is.

I don't care how good looking you are, unless you're truly a lovely person to be around, then you're not the ultimate prize of anyone. And, being a lovely person involves not thinking in such an egotistical manner. Therefore, these two concepts completely repel each other.

"It's Wrong to Be Interested in a Stranger"

There are many people who experience a type of shame about even the very idea of flirting, expressing sexual interest, or just talking to somebody they are interested in. The core of this thinking is the idea that sex is inherently wrong. I've also met men who believe any type of pursuit of a woman amounts to sexual harassment.

Sexual harassment is a hot-button topic (and for some reason that I don't understand, seems to be only relevant if it's *men* harassing *women*, but never the other way around). What constitutes it, and what doesn't? The answer is if she's smiling along with you and laughing; then a negative situation will obviously not arise. If, however, she feels uncomfortable and you don't get the social cues, I'd suggest to cut out the innuendos, flirts, teases.

Is there a small percentage of mentally unbalanced women who might scream sexual harassment and get you fired because you smiled at her while you got coffee? Yes. Such a pathology may develop as a result of childhood abuse and a fear of intimacy. But the vast majority of women are not this way.

Sex is never something to be ashamed of. And you're not some boorish freak for expressing your interest. It may take a while to deprogram these feelings from your head, but it's necessary if you intend to enhance your love life and obtain the confidence to approach a stranger with interest.

Chapter Summary

We explored a lot of mental concepts in this chapter. Emotional health, limiting beliefs, and philosophy are such deep topics that spans across so many categories, but they're also very important aspects of the human experience.

You must be very mindful about your own mental rhetoric; for it makes the difference not only between your success at dating, but the long-term success of your relationships—not just with your lovers, but in all of life, as well.

In regard to dating, the takeaway point here is to separate a quest for power from a quest for love and romance. Too often in western culture, these two points become intermixed, and dating becomes an ego-based activity. And as we know, the ego can never be fully satisfied.

Chapter Six – Online Dating Ins and Outs

It's important to talk about online dating because it's a common default option that we elect when we otherwise do not feel like leaving the house. I'm going to run through some of the online options, and discuss the merits and (obvious) major downsides to it. However, I won't simply rant about the vices of this strategy, and I'll try to provide some useful knowledge to do it correctly. Meeting people online IS possible, if you know some secrets.

The Immediate Problem With Online Dating

The shy types and introverts flock to this medium. It provides an immediate outlet to socialize *without really socializing*. Truly, the internet is the great phenomenon of the ages; something that Generation Y will surely take for granted. In days before the internet, there was never an option for mass communication with strangers. Everyone was forced to interact physically, or not at all.

As I believe social skills are developed and practiced, the internet is something you need to take a breather from. While communicating online is easy, it does not take into account factors like body language. Video chat and Skype may assist with this, but it's still not the same as in-person interaction.

That being said, online dating is still a (sometimes) fun way to meet people. It allows you to potentially score a date without doing that much work. You simply create your profiles, leave them alone, and check for new messages from time to time. It basically increases your chances in a passive way.

However, relying on internet dating is a mistake, for the reasons I will now cover:

The Online Dating Landscape

In Western countries in particular, online dating is a peculiar reflection of the dating landscape. Online dating has a lot of oddities, like how it tends to favor women—in a way that I recently verified through an experiment.

I created two profiles in the Los Angeles area, using the popular free dating resource Plenty of Fish. For my profile photos I used some all-purpose royalty free images I found of attractive looking people. Not bombshells or sex symbols, just regular happy people (with the exception of their very nice teeth).

On the male side, we had Brad:

Brad enjoys sports, mountain climbing, sledding, good food, long hikes, and cuddling by the fire. He makes about $45,000 a year and owns a small condo. He is 6'0.

On the female side, meet Sarah:

Sarah is a dental assistant who makes close to Brad's salary. She enjoys yoga, meditation, sports, video games, camping, and (also) cuddling. Aren't these guys made for each other?

I ensured each fake profile answered their same amount of questions, to guarantee they had the same amount of match possibilities. When everything was finished, I simply waited to see what would happen.

After a one month period:

Brad: 1 message
Sarah: 143 messages

(If you don't believe me and you have too much time on your hands, try this experiment yourself. You'll get the same results. Using a slightly more attractive female avatar, I've heard of people yielding as many as 500 to even 1,000 messages per month).

I don't want to be too hard on myself or others by using Brad as some type of standard, but the average guy out there isn't him. I don't play many sports and I rent instead of own. In addition, I'm not six foot. On a good day, I'm near 5'10—most days, 5'9. Plus, there's no way I'm as photogenic as he is.

And yet, even Brad was completely ignored in comparison to Sarah, who by all accounts is a fairly normal woman. Not a celebrity, not a supermodel. Yet, she would still get messaged 4-5 time per day. Why?

Some psychologists would argue it's because men will sooner feel attracted based on the visual stimuli. Men are wired to seek after pretty girls, and as soon as they feel attracted their finger moves to the mouse button. By comparison, a woman is more likely to be emotionally and logically attuned to attraction.

Sociologically, one could argue it's because of a culture that tells men that the masculine thing to do is to be the pursuer of women. That it's a woman's job to be a selector, and a man's job to seek. In the West, these roles are exacerbated, and is possibly combined with a general abundance of lonely males compared to less-lonely females.

The end result of this phenomenon is that many women on dating sites have a flood of options at their door, every single day. While this number greatly decreases if the woman is middle-aged or older, or appears overweight, she will still receive more messages than the average male *in his prime* by at least a 3:1 ratio (source: further testing I later did).

Because of so many options, it's safe to assume that women begin sorting men based on even shallow criteria. And, I don't blame them; how else can you deal with the barrage of attention? You have to somehow create a sorting mechanism for the purposes of saving time.

It may look something like: "Dark hair, check, high income, check, tall, check, nice smile, check", you get the idea.

"But Cyrus, there can only be so many men in the world who fit that bill!"

Yes, and those "perfect guys" who also happen to have online dating profiles make up about 90% of the dates that women go on. When dealing with the online game, my studies have shown that most female attention gets funneled into small group of men who have the most striking profiles. Lucky bastards, right?

And Herein Lies the Problem With Online Dating

For women, online dating becomes a game of whack-a-mole. They keep messaging you, and as if using a mallet to whack moles, you continually X out of those windows.

In real life, for a man to approach you he needs two things: courage and legitimate interest in you. Online it just takes boredom and happy fingers (plus maybe general horniness). So, as men send their daily bouts of endless e-mails, you'll start trying to sort them all based on a formula. When you finally find a man who's not: nerdy, skinny, fat, pale, short, insecure, not confident looking, doesn't look like your ex, bad fashion sense, and so forth—you'll find out he's not very serious, and possibly a player (as every other woman is messaging him too, and he's certainly enjoying himself).

For men, you could pretty much have your shit together in life, and be gifted with good looks to boot, and like poor Brad find yourself in a desert with zero attention. You may start to wonder "Wow, is there something wrong with me—is it my large nose?"

And, in fact, it MAY be your large nose. Poor Brad had a bit of a big schnoz, and I wouldn't be surprised at all if that was a limiting factor. Again, women are using sorting mechanisms, and like a casting director overrun with auditions, it doesn't take much to not make the cut.

A System of Appearances: Is It Worth It?

Therefore the grim reality of online dating is that it's a very visual thing. And the more the dating system relies on first impression via profile pic, the more you will be stuck as a slave to such criteria.

The least visual online dating system could be a paid site like Match.com that pairs people based on a lot of psychological criteria. By contrast the most visual (and worst) would be an app like Tinder, where you simply sweep to the left to reject somebody based on whatever split-second impression you get.

For a male entering this arena, my advice is very shallow. Here it is:

- Show off your best features.
- So if you have abs, it's time to go shirtless by the pool.
- If you have abs but you're very pale, better get a tan first.
- If you have a tan but you don't have abs, well—you get the idea.
- Show you're fun. Make profile pics around friends and at parties. They don't have to know that on most Friday nights you're playing old Nintendo 64 games in your underwear.
- Avoid mentioning deal breakers. Never put "I'd rather not say" as an answer, because it really means something bad. So if your income is "I'd rather not say", you may as well be saying $7,000 a year part-time at Taco Bell.

- Try to be edgy and "cool" somehow. If your greatest asset is a striped polo shirt, try rocking some designer sunglasses. If you're bald and look like a Q-tip, try a manly goatee.

For a woman, it's a three-fold process:

- Post an attractive photo of yourself.
- Exist.
- Pick a lovable loser out of the endless inquiries.

Do you feel kind of disgusted yet? That's a natural feeling. That's how I feel about online dating, as well. I realize you may have found some of these observations surprising or even absurd. I feel the same way. But these are not just my opinions—it's the unfortunate truth about how this medium plays out the majority of the time.

Why Meeting in Person is Superior

Because online dating is a visual game, you're missing out on what really makes people attracted to each other. In real life, it's neither a logical process based on criteria that the old happy dude from the eHarmony commercials figured out, nor is it about a bit of sexual fantasy from viewing someone's picture.

As a man, if you are very confident, regardless of whether you have abs or any other goofy standard, a woman can feel head-over-heels attracted to you. She will feel attracted based on how you present yourself, your body language, how you smell, how you look at her, how you talk to her.

For women, these same things apply, too. In fact, a woman may attract a man based on her bikini photo online, only to discover that same man may not want anything to do with her in person—once he discovers how she looks at him, how she talks, how she carries herself, etc.

I think this is great news for a lot of us. Real attraction has such little to do with appearances or those genetic factors that are out of our control, and so much to do with hidden elements of chemistry.

I've met many men in my life, from college on through the real world, who feel completely overwhelmed because of online dating standards. They become self-conscious, obsessed with working out, and develop body dysmorphic disorders. They may also acquire other unhealthy tendencies from jealousy to even misogynistic feelings.

It's not necessary. Don't let this happen to you.

How Online Dating Can Actually Work

You may have surmised at this point that I don't recommend making an online dating profile, in particular if you're a guy. If you're a girl, it might be worth trying out—but don't let it go to your head.

There are, however, solutions to help you meet people online that does not involve $39.99 a month subscriptions or trying to take a photo where you look like a male model.

The answer lies with groups and communities. Namely, I've had the most luck with Facebook groups.

These should be communities that you are actively a part of, and that you make posts and share ideas on.

I prefer topics related to things like health, fitness, science, esoteric studies, meditation, consciousness, etc. I find smarter groups, or groups that attract people who are fit and healthy, are far more likely to bring in a higher quality of subscriber. Avoid places where people debate and fight incessantly; for instance political groups. If you can find a group that's local, even better. You may try searching Facebook for <name of your city> and <hiking, health, fitness, discussion, book club> or whatever else interests you.

When I look back at my life, I realize I've had a lot of luck meeting people this way. Sometimes, I forget they're people that I ultimately met online, because it felt as natural as meeting them anywhere else.

By contrast, I have never successfully cracked the dating website thing. My profile on PoF is even worse than Brad's—it's a total wasteland.

This is not to say you may not have more luck online dating, and again—if you're a lady—you'll probably get more attention than you can stand. However, for us guys who are not magnanimously impressive, it's going to be a rough tide to be able to date with any degree of selectivity.

Chapter Seven – Help, I Still Can't Find a Date!

When everything's said and done, many of us still have problems finding those dates. Instead of beating yourself up about it, let's explore some of the common reasons why you've been loveless for the last year and a half.

Think of this chapter as the problem-solving portion. Refer to it when you feel stuck elsewhere.

You're staying at home too much.

As pleasant as it is to stay at home and unwind after work, it's not going to push your social life forward very far. You might just not be trying to leave your house enough. Refer to my suggestions earlier in this book about certain groups and activities.

You won't approach people.

So, you found a cool mixer at some outdoor venue. You arrive, dressed up, and you leave after stirring a drink for an hour. That's how we shy, introverted types may behave by default. You must go outside of your comfort zone and instead work to talk to as many people as you can.

Your mood and energy levels are low.

Remember what I said before about energy levels? Your energy is going to affect the mood of people around you. Avoid heavy foods, simple carbs, and caffeine before you go socialize. Make sure you've had plenty of rest, and that you feel in a generally positive mood.

You overwhelm strangers.

What topics are you talking about? Are you telling strangers about your problems? Are you dumping emotional waste on them? Very bad idea. Reconsider your types of conversations. Keep things directed more toward them instead of you. Ask open-ended questions.

You're extremely serious.

Not everyone grows a funny bone overnight, but you can at least lighten things up by not choosing only serious, boring topics. Politics, Islamic extremists, ebola. Get off those threads and find literally anything lighthearted as an alternative.

You eject too fast.

You won't get to know someone or be able to comfortably get their digits and stay in contact by running away very fast. Push yourself to keep talking. Circle around the room and find the same people again, and gauge the situation. If they seem responsive to you, with positive body language, don't be afraid to seek a table together with that person or maybe go take a walk to the balcony. The point is, try to keep something going! Shyness loves to manifest by making you say "goodbye" too fast. Resist.

You don't read social cues.

If someone is sending negative body language signs and is not demonstrating they are attracted to you, then don't keep trying to push it and make something work. It won't. Find someone who appears interested and let that other person go.

You don't develop the relationships.

When you have their contact info, then what? Whether it's a person you're already in constant contact with through your social circle, or it's a stranger—you need to develop the relationship by talking to them—and talking to them frequently. If you don't call back the phone-numbers you get, make plans, or stay in touch through any medium (even online), then the relationship will remain at a stand-still.

You're not flirting.

If you desire to *date* versus make friends, then that new stranger in your life must get the sense almost immediately that you're interested in something more. This may include flirtatious body language or making a move and going for a kiss. The sooner this is established, the better—with the very best time to establish it the moment that you meet someone. The longer you wait, the harder it will become.

You want it too badly.

This may sound odd, but understand that in the world of human relationships, desiring something too much will project a type of neediness. A person who is comfortable in their own skin sees relationships with other people as complimentary to their own selves—NOT as something they pin their entire happiness on.

Life is hard and full of tragedies. From unexpected illnesses that kill the people we love, to crippling injuries. There is no shortage of great tests and hurdles to go through. And so, it becomes easy to feel one must lean on the support of others just to get through life on a day to day basis.

If, however, you are entirely reliant on others for happiness, many risks come with that—namely, emotional codependency disorders. At the end of the day, and as this book nears its finish point, what I want you to consider is that your relationship with yourself is of primary importance.

If in any way you feel uncertain in your own skin, it is something that must be resolved. If you feel self-conscious about your appearance, if you feel shame about something you did in your past, or if you feel unworthy compared to other people—these are all things that must be figured out as a prerequisite to dating.

The healthiest relationships occur when two people fully trust themselves and their emotions. When they come from a position of seeking others to compliment them.

Whenever you hear mainstream advice or hallmark cards with notions of "You complete me" or "you're my other half", run away. This is social brainwashing at work. In no relationship should another person "complete" you. You must already be complete and secure with yourself. A relationship where one person completes the other is, in my eyes, a codependency situation waiting to happen.

The dating phase is an excellent point to immediately ensure that you are not only happy in your own skin, but you're meeting other happy people on the same vibration as you.

Love yourself first, before you ever try to seek intimate relationships.

Chapter Eight – Dating Worst Case Scenario Checklist

Dating can be an unpredictable thing. As human beings are, in fact, quite unpredictable and weird. You may run into certain strange situations, and I thought I'd compile a few of them, plus appropriate strategies you can take if they happen to you.

- Date Shows Up With Chaperone

What Happens: You schedule to meet a person (usually it's the guy meeting the girl), and she has her sister with her. The sister remains awkward and quiet the whole time. The date feels weird.

What it Means: This is either because you scheduled a date without building any rapport, such as a random internet date, or because the person in question has trust issues.

What to Do: In some cases this behavior can be very inappropriate. Like if you've already established a friendship and you're meeting in a public space. In such a situation this could be a sign that she had some traumatic incident happen to her in her past and she's not quite over it. You have every right to either call the date off or be blunt about asking if her sister is a chaperone, and why she doesn't feel comfortable. If she's assumes every man she meets is a rapist, you're going to be in for a lot of other issues as you get to know her.

- Date is Not the Same as Online Profile

What Happens: Your date looks a lot different than the pic you saw, usually for the negative. This happens on both sides of the gender aisle. In the struggle for men to appear date worthy (see chapter six), they may embellish themselves to be more appealing. Women certainly do this as well, by shooting the perfect angle where they look thin and 10 years younger.

What it Means: A high level of self-consciousness and inability to think things through. If your profile pic is inaccurate, how do they expect it's just going to slide when the other person finds out?

What to Do: Call it off. Simply point out that the person was being deceptive, and wave goodbye (whether they respond with anger or not is their problem). Sorry you had to go through such an awkward experience. Stop messing around with dating sites.

- Date Tries to Kiss You and Fails

What Happens: Most often this relates to a guy with a girl. He will lean in for the kiss at an inappropriate time, and you will react by suddenly recoiling. Extreme awkwardness follows.

What it Means: He was trying his best, going on a limb, and he likely feels intense shame now. He was, at least, committed to escalating the date and not landing in friend zone. He just wasn't sure when and how to do it.

What to Do: Assess the situation. Understand he feels bad now. But, do you like him? Do you feel attracted to him? The thing he would most like to feel is forgiveness, and the best way to forgive a man for screwing up the kiss-timing is to put your hands around his face and kiss him! If, however, you really don't like him—then this would be a good time to call the date off and move onward.

- Date Projects Extremely "Creepy" Vibe

What Happens: You met someone, you think that person is cool, but upon a one on one meeting they seem very overwhelming, are trying to move too fast, and are maybe emotionally unstable.

What it Means: The person has some issues going on. One must worry about potential stalkers. Stalking occurs when somebody places undo value upon you; seeing you as a conquest, or fantasizing that their life would be perfect if you would accept and love them. This is usually a projection of childhood insecurities, abandonment complexes, and media induced brainwashing.

What to Do: Always meet people in public venues. Trust your instincts. Avoid meeting somebody in their home. Gauge the situation. Don't make later plans. Have a way out (you're going to a barmitzvah later). Don't spend your life worried every person you meet is a potential rapist, because most people are not and that paranoia will consume you. At the same time, be alert to warning signs and practice basic caution, including not giving out your home address or even your full name until you get to know a person better (and that includes adding the person on Facebook, where all the information is revealed).

- My Date Appears Displeased, But I Like Him / Her!

What Happens: You're having a good time, perhaps you feel attracted to the person, but he or she seems to be growing disinterested and bored by you. You don't know what you're doing wrong, but you have a crushing sense there won't be a second chance.

What it Means: The interest is not being reciprocated, which means you may be showing too much interest, too fast—and the personality type you're with gets turned off by this. You might be leaning in too much, showing too much affection, being caught up in their every word, complimenting a lot, and so forth.

What to Do: Immediately stop all positive body language, and cease attempts at flirting. Resume humor and teasing, but relax on appearing so goo-goo ga-ga. They'll understand that there was a shift. Certain people respond much better to "not caring". Generally, these are the types of people who prefer to win someone over versus have everything handed to them. And so, this is the one and only time a person should "play hard to get". Overall, though, if you're actually not compatible with this person, it may be best if there really are no second chances.

Final Thoughts

We have arrived at the conclusion of "Love and Dating for Shy People". The game of courtship has certainly evolved over the millennia, but some things stay the same, including the feeling of butterflies in our stomachs when we try to approach a member of the opposite sex.

As shy people, we have no excuse to hold ourselves back by believing the label of introversion has any real merit. Socializing is an art form and a skill that can be acquired, and as with any skill—with enough practice, an individual can achieve a sense of confidence at it.

As this confidence develops, you'll obtain more options for your love life. More people to date, and an easier time not only meeting new faces, but taking the necessary steps we all have to make to begin dating someone; from flirting to making the first move.

Today, socializing in general has become more laborious. Because of social media, it's harder to convince the average person to go out of the house. Therefore, it almost seems like tendencies toward shyness have increased. While technology is a great blessing on our lives, it's important to be reminded not to allow it to provide a sense of plausible deniability to stay indoors.

Hopefully, with these newfound skills, you will no longer have to rely on things like dating websites or "luck" to find new partners. The whole process becomes a lot easier when you're the one in control of your own destiny.

Related Books by Cyrus Thomson

As you may have guessed, I am always trying to brainstorm new ideas. Here are more programs from this series that I'd suggest to check out. Simply plug any of the following titles into Amazon.com:

30 Day Social Anxiety Bootcamp: Just like the title suggests. If you can't even leave your house because other people frighten you, I suggest a specific program to deal with social anxiety.

Alpha Confidence For Men and Women: Everyone always talks about having confidence as the most attractive factor, but what IS confidence? This book is designed to boost your sex appeal.

How to End a Relationship: Sometimes a date leads to a relationship, and sometimes that relationship needs to end.

Ultimate Men's Dating Advice Book: A similar program but tailored specifically for men.

How to Become a Powerful, Sexy Man: Another book for the guys. This one is about getting your life in order and becoming the guy a lot of women want to date.

Free E-Book and Newsletter

Don't forget to check out the free lifestyle e-book and newsletter with Developed Life Publishing. You can get started at www.developedlife.com. I look forward to hearing from you. Once you're on the newsletter, feel free to write me a line.

About the Author

Cyrus Thomson is originally from Arizona. He graduated from the University of Arizona in 2010 and then pursued a lifestyle as a world-traveler, before settling into Los Angeles and developing a successful career in writing and relationship-dating coaching. He has written numerous best-selling Amazon titles that explore everything from the roles of masculinity; dating, to business, marketing and psychology.

Made in United States
North Haven, CT
16 June 2025

69886127R00065